Complete
Handyman
do-it-yourself
Encyclopedia

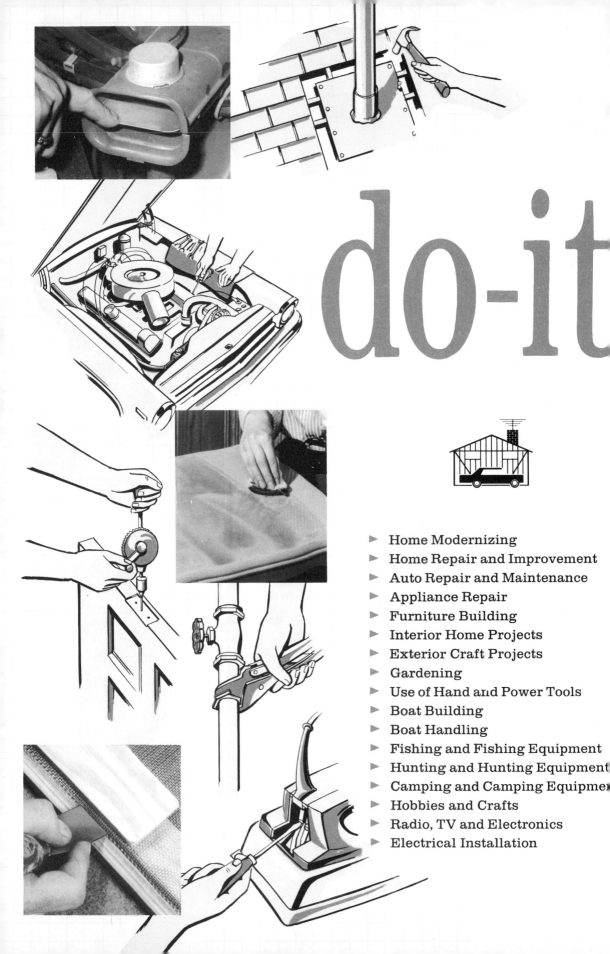

do-it

- Home Modernizing
- Home Repair and Improvement
- Auto Repair and Maintenance
- Appliance Repair
- Furniture Building
- Interior Home Projects
- Exterior Craft Projects
- Gardening
- Use of Hand and Power Tools
- Boat Building
- Boat Handling
- Fishing and Fishing Equipment
- Hunting and Hunting Equipment
- Camping and Camping Equipment
- Hobbies and Crafts
- Radio, TV and Electronics
- Electrical Installation

Complete
Handyman
yourself
Encyclopedia

A COMPILATION OF NEW AND PREVIOUSLY PUBLISHED SPECIAL
INTEREST PROJECTS AND MANUALS FOR THE
REPAIR AND CARE OF HOMES, AUTO,
APPLIANCES, HOBBY EQUIPMENT.
by the editors of

Science &
Mechanics

1

ABRASIVES
AUTOMOBILE ENGINES

H. S. STUTTMAN INC. *publishers*   Westport, CT.   06889

PRINTED IN THE UNITED STATES OF AMERICA

24P (0475) 100-2085R

INTRODUCTION

MODERN SCIENCE AND TECHNOLOGY have surrounded us with a vast assortment of products whose proper function affect our daily lives. Our homes, our automobiles, all our appliances, as well as our hobby and recreational equipment are the end result of applied science and technology and we take it for granted that these products will always function properly. Therefore, we are invariably annoyed when a malfunction deprives us of their use and enjoyment.

This annoyance becomes more aggravated when even minor repairs and adjustments are difficult to obtain and result in constantly increasing costs. The words "do-it-yourself" have, therefore, become of utmost importance when applied to maintaining and increasing the value, comfort, beauty and performance of practically everything you own or hope to acquire.

THE COMPLETE HANDYMAN "DO-IT-YOURSELF" ENCYCLOPEDIA represents the combined efforts of the writers, editors and technical consultants of Science & Mechanics magazine. With this authoritative background, these volumes can provide the "how-to" answers to practically any question pertaining to mechanical techniques and crafts.

In this new work, the authors have demonstrated that a reader can be motivated with the desire and equipped with the knowledge to "do-it-yourself." With just a few basic tools (skilled craftsmen even show you how to use them), the reader acquires confidence to:

construct a cabinet . . . change a spark plug . . . catch a bass

ceramic tile a countertop . . . refinish a chair . . . navigate a boat

paint a car . . . grow a bonsai garden . . . waterproof a cellar

install a bathroom . . . repair a carburetor . . . reload a shot shell

make a storm window . . . tile a floor . . . install electric outlets

maintain a pool . . . tune an engine . . . expand a room

The wide range and diversity of projects and techniques is amply demonstrated in the accompanying Table of Contents. This skillful combination of practical projects with instructions in the craft techniques for completing these projects is what the COMPLETE HANDYMAN DO-IT-YOURSELF ENCYCLOPEDIA is about. The reader quickly discovers, or gradually develops, basic skills as he becomes familiar with the craft techniques that help execute each project. Simplified, yet authoritative and jargon-free, instructions are combined with informative step-by-step self-teaching illustrations that encourage the reader to acquire new skills and improve on those he already has. Because the reader is exposed to this wide diversity of *attainable* projects, he is motivated to refine and improve on his methods for creating, building and repairing. The fun and enjoyment in each project is heightened in the knowledge of the substantial savings that have been effected.

The reader's attention is called to legal and safety aspects to many of the licensed crafts which prompt the editors to include a warning note. Some community local laws and regulations prohibit anyone but licensed professionals from doing certain jobs. In such cases, a practical knowledge of the craft enables the reader to better evaluate both the cost and quality of work performed.

To make this set more useful to the reader, and to encourage browsing and using each volume as a source of ideas, four cross referenced aids are provided. The alphabetic headings at the top of each page cover broad classifications of projects and techniques. The caption underneath each heading is the title of a project, craft or technique that may logically fall within this alphabetic heading. At the end of most articles "See also" references direct the reader to other articles dealing with the same general subject under another alphabetic entry. Alphabetic cross references shown at the bottom of a page call attention to an article that appears under another alphabetic heading. A complete alphabetic Index by subjects and topics is contained in the back section of Volume 21 and will provide aid in quickly locating information within any topic.

In producing this work, the authors were fortunate in having the advice and guidance of Mr. Joel Davis, President and Publisher of SCIENCE & MECHANICS PUBLICATIONS, INC. The publishers wish to express their gratitude for his assistance and admiration for his dedication to the task of showing readers how to "do-it-yourself."

Shortly after the first edition reached its audience, an analysis of reader requests revealed a desire for expanded *step-by-step guides to successful vegetable and fruit growing*. The GROW YOUR OWN step-by-step growing guides in Volumes 22 to 26, with their full-color illustrations, were designed to give fast answers and advice on every gardening question. GROW YOUR OWN is an authoritative, foolproof guide to gardening success. Edited by Edwin F. Steffek, famed garden authority, author and former editor of Horticulture Magazine. The addition of these volumes makes this Handyman Encyclopedia truly "complete."

H. S. STUTTMAN CO., INC.
PUBLISHERS

CONTRIBUTORS

Initials at end of articles identify the author

M.C.A.	M. C. Anderson	H.R.G.	H. R. Gleyre
F.J.B.	F. J. Bauer	T.G.	Townsend Godsey
D.B.	Dave Beatie	K.G.	Ken Grant
B.B.	Bob Behme	T.H.	Thomas Hardman
R.L.B.	Robert Lee Behme	M.H.	Marvin Harper
R.B.	Ron Benrey	B.H.	Bill Hartford
F.B.	Fred Blakemore	F.H.	Frank Hegemeyer
G.B.	George Bodmer	L.H.	Lou Heiner
L.M.B.	Lillian M. Borgeson	M.A.H.	Margaret Herbst
T.B.	Thomas Bottomley	R.H.	Robert Hertzberg
R.A.B.	Raymond Bridge	O.E.H.	O. E. Hopper
J.B.	Jacklyn Buboltz	C.R.H.	Clinton R. Hull
L.B.	Len Buckwalter	J.H.	Jorma Hyypia
J.C.	John Capotosto	H.F.J.	Herman F. Johnson
F.C.C., JR.	Fred C. Clark, Jr.	S.J.	Sam Julty
F.C.	Frank Cogan	H.K.	Hal Kelly
M.C.	Marley Cole	J.K.	John Krill
P.A.C.	Paul Corey	E.P.K.	Emil P. Kushner
H.K.C.	H. K. Cox	E.P.K., SR.	Emil P. Kushner, Sr.
N.C.	Norman Crawford	G.L.	George Laycock
P.C.	Pete Czura	R.F.L.	Robert F. Lewis
B.W.D.	Byron W. Dalrymple	R.L.	Ray Lorenz
G.D.	George Daniels	E.M.L.	Edwin M. Love
H.L.D.	Homer L. Davidson	T.M.C.	Ted McCawley
R.J.D.	R. J. DeCristoforo	G.M.C.	Gordon McComb
R.D.	Richard Dietz	T.M.	Ted Mann
M.E.D.	M. E. Dowd	J.M.	Jim Martenhoff
J.D.	John Duffett	F.M.	Frank Martin
D.D.	Dave Duffey	A.M.	Anthony Mastey
M.E.	Milt Evans	C.R.M.	Charles R. Meyer
T.F.	Tom Faulkner	G.M.	George Meyerink
B.F.	Bob Fendell	E.M.	Ellison Michel
M.E.F.	Mark E. Fineman	S.M.M.	Stephen M. Miller
H.F.	Herbert Friedman	W.G.M.	Willis G. Misch
M.F.	Marv Frydenlund	E.A.M.	Edward A. Morris
I.G.	Imre Georgenvi	G.E.M.	Gordon E. Morrison
J.G.	Jerry Gibbs	L.M.	Les Morrow

B.M.	Burt Murphy
M.N.	Martin Nolsen
J.O.	Joseph Olivari
P.P.	Pat Perrett
F.P.	Fred Petras
T.P.	Tom Philbin
R.G.P.	R. G. Puckett
C.D.R.	Charles D. Rakes
N.R.	N. Raskhodoff
A.N.R.	Alexander N. Retsoff
J.L.R.	Judith L. Reynolds
C.R.	Chuck Richards
V.H.R.	Victor H. Ries
S.R.	Stanley Rosenfeld
R.S.	Robert Scharff
D.S.	Don Shiner
P.K.S.	Patrick K. Snook
J.S.	Jack Speirs
J.R.S.	James R. Squires
H.S.	Harry Stavert
B.S.	Bob Steindler
E.M.S.	Eleanor M. Stothart
H.P.S.	Harold P. Strand
A.S.	Andy Sugar
D.M.S.	David M. Swartwout
B.T.	Bill Thomas
J.B.T.	Jack B. Thornton
A.T.	Arthur Trauffer
R.T.	Ralph Treves
P.W.A.	Paul Wahl
C.F.W.	Charles F. Waterman
D.W.	David Weems
P.W.	Paul Weissler
R.W.	Robin White
G.L.W.	Glen L. Witt
J.W.	James Wyckoff
A.Y.	Alan Young

CONTENTS

BOAT HANDLING

CANOE

3

CARBURETORS

CLUTCH

4

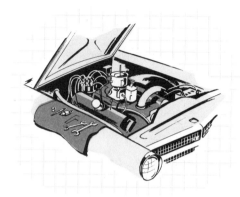

COFFEE MAKERS

DESKS

5

DIMMER, LIGHT

6

ELECTRICITY

ELECTRIC RANGE

7

FIREPLACE

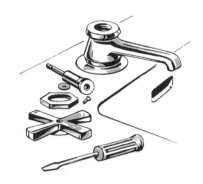

FIREWOOD

GARAGE REMODELING   8

GARDENING
HOME IMPROVEMENT

9

HOME INSULATION
LASER

10

LATHE
MODEL CAR LAYOUT

11

MOLDINGS
PAINT SPRAYERS

12

PANELS
PICTURE FRAMING

13

PLASTICS, FABRICATING
REPAIRS, AUTOMOBILE

14

ROOFS

SCIENCE PROJECTS

15

SCREENS

SPARK PLUG

16

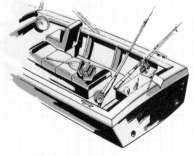

SWIMMING POOL

TOOLS

18

TOOLS, GARDEN

UPHOLSTERY

19

VACUUM CLEANER

20

WILDLIFE

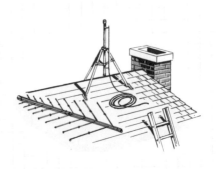

WIND GAUGE

INDEX

21

CREDITS

In striving to make this publication as complete, accurate and up to date as possible a great deal of assistance and technical information was obtained from manufacturers trade association and governmental agencies. The editors are deeply grateful to all of them for their help and wish to thank the following organizations for the illustrations they have made available:

AMF Swimaster
Airstream, Inc.
Allied International Films Ltd.
American Olean Tile Company
American Plywood Association
Apeco Recreational Vehicles
Armstrong Cork Company
Aromatic Red Cedar Closet Lining Manufacturers Association
Arrow Fastener Co., Inc.
Baths International, Inc.
Behr-Manning
Black and Decker Manufacturing Company
Boy Scouts of America
The Brewster Corporation
W. Atlee Burpee Co.
Champion Spark Plug Company
Dayton Products, Inc.
The Decro-Wall Corporation
Disston, Inc.
Dow Chemical U.S.A.
Dupont Building Products
Dupont Paint Company
Eastman Kodak Company
Emhart Corporation
Enertech
Environmental Science Service Administration
Filon Division of Vistron Corporation
Florida News Bureau
Fluidmaster
Four Seasons Greenhouses
Frigid, Inc.
Frigidaire Division General Motors Corp.
GTE Sylvania, Inc.
General Electric Company
Georgia-Pacific Corporation
Glen L. Marine
Hartline Products Co., Inc.
Homelite A Textron Division
The Hoover Company
Hotpoint
Hunt Manufacturing Company

In-Sink-Erator Division, Emerson Electric Company
Interlux
International Paint Company
JFD Electronics Corporation
Jackson & Perkins
Jacobs Wind Electric Co.
Johnson Motors Division of Outboard Marine Corp.
Jotul U.S.A.
Kenwood Stereo
Lecomar, Inc.
Malak Photographs, Ltd.
Masonite Corporation
The Maytag Company
Mazda Motors of America, Inc.
Mercury Marine
Meridian Yachts
Michigan Tourist Council
Mineral Insulation Manufacturers Association
Benjamin Moore and Company
Nashua Stoves
National Swimming Pool Institute
Nebraska Game Commission
New York State College of Agriculture and Life Sciences
New York State College of Human Ecology
Northern Stone Supply, Inc.
NuTone Division, Scovill Housing Products Group
Oakridge Industries
Old Town Co.
Owens-Corning Fiberglass Corp.
Ozite Corporation
Pioneer Electronics of America
Pittsburgh Paint Company
Pittway Corporation
Plastronics, Inc.
Plexiglas
Portland Cement Association
Power Tool Institute, Inc.
Quaker Manufacturing Company
RCA
RCBS Incorporated
Red Devil, Inc.

Reynolds Aluminum
Rockwell Manufacturing Company Power Tool Division
Rohm and Haas Company
Morris Rosenfeld & Sons
Sanyo Electric, Inc.
School Products Co., Inc.
Schwinn Bicycle Company
Set Products
Sharon Communications, Inc.
Sherwin-Williams Paint Company
Simpson Timber Company
Solahart California
Solar Resources, Inc.
The Sony Corporation
Stanley Door Systems
Stanley Power Tools Division of The Stanley Works
The Stanley Works
Sunbeam Appliance Company
The Swan Corporation
Swim Gard, Inc.
Swingline, Inc.
Switchpack Systems, Inc.
Texas Parks and Wildlife Department
3M Company
Tibbals Flooring Company
Tile Council of America
True Temper Corporation
United Gilsonite Laboratories
U. S. Coast Guard
U. S. Department of Agriculture
U. S. Forest Service
United States Gypsum
U. S. Plywood Division of Champion International
Wallcovering Industry Bureau, Inc.
Watco-Dennis Corp.
Western Wood Products Association
Wheeler, Knight & Gainey, Inc.
Wilson Imperial
Winnebago Industries, Inc.
J. Wiss & Sons Co.
York Division, Borg-Warner Corp.

Steve Ellingson construction projects appear through the courtesy of UB Newspaper Syndicate, 15125 Saticoy St., Van Nuys, Cal. 91409.

VOLUME 1

What You Should Know about Abrasives

How to choose and use old standbys like sandpaper, plus new buffing and polishing materials

Non-woven synthetic fiber pads impregnated with abrasive particles for finish sanding, scouring, etc. Colors indicate the coarseness grade.

WHETHER YOU CALL IT SANDPAPER or coated abrasive, it's the same thing and it does the same jobs. The readily available abrasive types are five in number. The one you use depends on the job to be done and the material involved.

There's a technique in using any of these abrasives to get the best result. To see the overall picture let's look at the abrasives first, then the methods of using them.

Flint, a natural abrasive, is the oldest of the common woodworking types still widely used. It has a short working life and relatively poor cutting power. But, being the lowest in price, it's a very popular type for work that clogs the abrasive quickly and requires frequent replacement, as in heavy paint removal. It is grayish white, but acquires a yellowish tinge from the adhesive that holds it to the paper backing. And, as it looks like sand, it can probably be credited with keeping alive the term "sandpaper." It is a good choice for small sanding jobs and any work that requires a cheap, throw-away abrasive.

Garnet is another natural abrasive. It has much sharper cutting edges (when crushed) than flint, and is much harder. So it cuts faster, lasts longer, and is a good low cost woodworking abrasive. It is easy to recognize by its red color—the same red color that makes large pieces attractive when faceted and polished for jewelry use.

Emery, also a natural abrasive, was once the major metal-finishing type. It is black, slow-cutting and short-lived. But, its rounded, slow-cutting crystals have very good polishing qualities that give it a lasting place in the workshop. It is also used by tradition-minded craftsman and by those unfamiliar with the more efficient artificial abrasives now available for cutting rather than polishing action.

Aluminum oxide, a reddish brown artificial abrasive, is perhaps the most versatile and widely used of the synthesized types. Being extremely tough and sharp, it is excellent for wood, metal, and the majority of other materials usually handled in the home workshop. It far outlasts any of the natural abrasives, and cuts much faster, though it costs somewhat more.

Silicon carbide, a blue-black artificial abrasive, is almost as hard as the diamond, and the sharpest of all five common abrasive types. But its crystals are too brittle

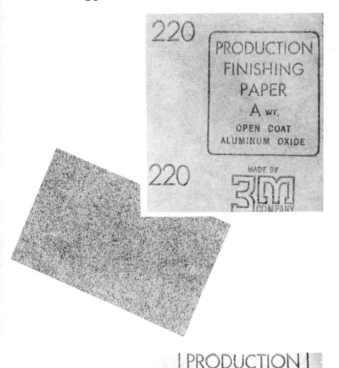

for general use on metals like iron and steel. It is a good choice, however, for softer metals like aluminum and bronze, because it cuts very fast without excessive speed or pressure. It also has ample strength for use on glass, and is widely used in glass work. It is the ideal abrasive, too, for many soft materials like leather. It is, in fact one of the leading abrasives in shoemaking and shoe repair.

All of these abrasives are readily available at hardware stores, though silicon carbide may not be stocked by some because of its more specialized applications. If you can't obtain it through local sources, contact an abrasive manufacturer for your nearest source of supply.

Pumice and rottenstone are natural abrasives not commonly available retail in coated abrasive form. They are obtainable, however, in fine powdered form through paint stores, and are widely used in producing the desired sheen in fine furniture work. The powder is mixed with No. 10 motor oil, or similar light oil, to make a creamy paste. (Water mixtures and others are sometimes used.) The technique of application is described later.

The coarseness of coated abrasives is measured in several ways, according to the type of the abrasive, its application, and to some extent, the market to which it is sold.

Industrial users, for example, prefer to specify coarseness by grit size—the minimum size sieve openings through which the

◀*Abrasive paper carries specification labels on back. Paper at top is 220 (finishing) grade, classed as "fine." Paper at bottom is 50 (coarse) grade. Grit numbers indicate number of holes per square inch in sieves through which particles are graded. "A wt." indicates weight of paper (light). "D wt." is heavy. Open coat indicates that abrasive particles are spaced out so only 50 to 70 percent of paper area is covered with abrasive. Objective: reduce clogging.*

abrasive grains will pass. (The extra fine and super fine sizes are graded by air flotation and water sedimentation processes.) An extra coarse abrasive might have a grit size of 16, extra fine might be as high 600 (each representing the number of sieve openings in a given area.)

Some users, on the other hand, still think in terms of the old symbol system, using 0, 2/0, 3/0, etc. And many home shop workers like the simplified terminology of extra fine, fine, medium, etc.

A coarseness grading term from at least one of these systems will be found printed on the back of your sandpaper (coated abrasive). The grit size is also printed on screen-backed abrasive. The non-woven pad types, however, usually have to be identified as to coarseness by color. Check on this where you buy unless you find the coarseness grade printed on the package.

The backing of coated abrasives is usually paper or cloth, though combinations are also used for special purposes. For most workshop applications a paper backing is the choice, with cloth backing reserved for heavy duty jobs, as in some forms of metal work. In general, lighter weight backings of either type are used with fine grit sizes for flexibility. Heavier backings go with coarser grits that are likely to be used under conditions of greater stress.

Open coat abrasive paper is made with abrasive grains separated by pre-set distances so that the abrasive covers only about 50 to 70 per cent of the surface. The gap between abrasive particles greatly reduces clogging with sanded material. This type can be used for most sanding work with a saving in time and expense, and is available from the usual sandpaper sources.

Wet-or-dry coated abrasive can be used with water or other liquids to wash away abraded material. Use it on car body work and other jobs requiring very fine abrasive that would be subject to frequent clogging.

Sanding methods depend on the job, and whether the work is done by hand or power. The number of different grades of coarseness the job requires depends on the initial roughness of the surface to be smoothed. If you are starting with rough wood, for example, as it might be after cutting to size on a workshop table saw, you would start sanding with a 50 or 60 grit size, sand with the grain, and continue until the entire surface has the same sanded texture. Then switch to a grit size of about 100. Work in stages to a finishing grit size around 220 or 240, never skipping more than one grit size when switching from one stage to the next. If the wood is smooth surfaced (as dressed lumber from the lumberyard) you can start with a grit size around 120. All this, assuming you want an extremely fine finish. After sanding, it is extremely important that all dust be removed from the work. Otherwise, dust specks will appear in whatever finish is applied.

As the finishing grit size used varies somewhat with the species and condition of the wood (seasoning, etc.) it helps to try the steps on a scrap if one is available. The final bare finish on some hardwoods can be improved by ending with a finer grade than would be required on the common soft woods. The finish applied to the wood must also be sanded between coats, preferably with very fine grit finishing paper in the 320 to 400 range. If your hardware store doesn't stock paper this fine you can get it from auto supply dealers, as it is used in auto body work. The final coat is not sanded.

In metal work the best abrasive in most instances is aluminum oxide. Use it to remove rust, starting with a coarseness suited to the roughness of the corrosion. Then work up to the final smoothing in stages, as with wood. To avoid frequent clogging of the abrasive, use an open coat type. On badly corroded surfaces a flexible disk sander on a power drill speeds the work greatly. Sanding disks are readily available in hardware stores in all the grit sizes likely to be needed. Do not expect to bring the metal to a mirror finish. An attractive satin type finish is usually obtainable, however. This makes a good base for painting.

Shaping with sandpaper is also easy with the aid of the flexible disk sander. The procedure is suited to many woodworking jobs, and is best carried out with aluminum oxide abrasive. As an example, if you have cut a toy boat hull to rough shape with a saber saw or compass saw, you can use the disk sander to provide the rounded contours.

The technique calls for keeping the disk moving over the areas to be shaped. The outer half of the disk radius does most of the work. Apply enough pressure to flex the disk slightly against the work. But do not apply enough pressure to slow the disk appreciably. High r.p.m. is best for fast cutting.

Practice on a scrap before tackling an actual project. Wear glasses or goggles during the work; abrasive grains that occasionally fly off the disk could injure the eyes.

Work up from coarse to fine, as in ordinary wood finishing, and the end product will be as smooth as conventional woodwork. On many jobs, the disk-shaping procedure does the job faster and better than any other tool.

Using a powdered abrasive, like pumice, is a simple matter. The purpose is the reduction of a high gloss to a softer sheen— desirable on many furniture projects. Mix the pumice (available from paint stores) with inexpensive No. 10 motor oil to form a creamy paste. Rub this paste over the work with a soft cloth and light pressure.

Wipe off the paste frequently to examine the effect. The pumice works fairly fast, and can cut through the finish if you go too far without stopping to check the results. Be careful along corners and on sharply rounded areas, because it is easy to apply too much pressure at such points and cut through the surface coating you are working on. With moderate care, however, the pumice and oil method produces very attractive results and is surprisingly easy. Wipe the finished job throroughly to remove all traces of the paste and oil residue.

Abrasive pads can do much the same job without the need for cleanup. Your best bet is to try the grades on a concealed area of the piece to be rubbed, starting with the finest. A minute of rubbing will usually tell the grade best suited to the job. Steel wool can be used for this purpose, too, but usually requires more work to produce equivalent results.

Power sanders are made in various basic types that should be matched, where possible, to the type of work. Some of the more versatile types can be used for a wide variety of jobs.

Reciprocal sanders operate with a back-and-forth motion, much like with-the-grain

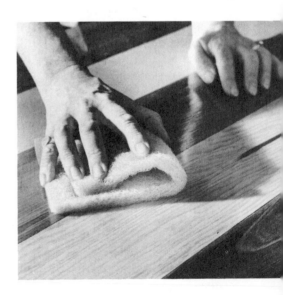

▶ *Rubbing down ribbon top table to give satin finish, using abrasive pad.*

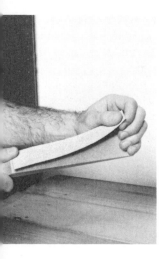

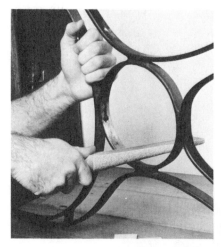

◄ *Multi-shaped sanding file simplifies sanding tight or sharp angles, curves and other hard-to-get-at surfaces in wood, metal and plastic. Just apply adhesive-backed sanding strip to file's surface and you have a very efficient abrasive.*

▼ *Use steel wool for dulling with minimum finish removal, also for cleaning, preparing for wax over finish. Twisted into cord form, it works in carvings, lathe turnings and similar forms.*

▼ *Abrasive on plastic screen has high degree of flexibility, comes in different coarseness grades (see text), and can be cut to size required. Use on contoured surfaces where paper backing can't conform.*

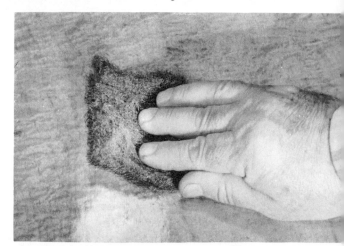

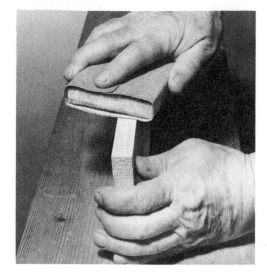

➤ *To sand to square cornered edge by hand, pull abrasive paper tightly around wood sanding block, sand with grain.*

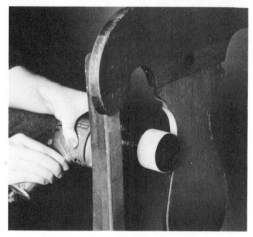

hand sanding. They do the same job as hand sanding, but do it faster. And they should be used with the same grit size stages as in hand sanding.

Orbital sanders (sometimes combined in dual types for selective reciprocal or orbital motion) move the sandpaper in a small rotary orbit. Instead of moving back and forth, the sandpaper combines a side motion, producing an "orbit" about ⅜" diameter. The orbital motion is very useful where the wood grain meets from several directions, as at a miter. Instead of sanding with the grain on one piece and crosswise on the other, as a reciprocal sander would, the orbital type sands with the same rotary motion on both pieces. Both this and the reciprocal type are good finishing sanders for most work.

◄ *Fast removal of old finishes from curved surfaces is no problem with a sanding wheel attached to a power drill. Wheel diameters are available in 4³/₈-, 2¹/₄-, and one-inch sizes. Adhesive backed sanding strips go on in seconds and stay on, no tools needed.*

► *More power sanders. Near right at top, a belt sander with dust collector. It is fast-cutting and good for big jobs on flat surfaces. Far right is a dual-action sander that moves sandpaper in a small rotary orbit. Bottom is a variable-speed power drill with disc sander attachment. Adhesive-backed sandpaper adheres to the disc quickly and efficiently. Good for rough work as well as rounding and shaping of wood.*

What You Should Know about Abrasives   *31*

The belt sander provides a uni-directional motion by means of an abrasive-coated belt that operates much as the treads of a bulldozer. Hence, it is essential to keep a good grip on the sander to keep it from "running away" across the work. The motors in these sanders are usually much more powerful than those in other types, and they are fast cutting when used with coarse grit belts. For the fastest cutting they are often used at a 45 degree angle across the wood grain, first in one direction, then the other. Final smoothing is with the grain.

Disk sanders are made in three basic types. The flexible disk sander, probably the most common and inexpensive, is simply a rubber disk with a center shaft for mounting in a power drill chuck, and a centered screw flange gripping the abrasive disk. This type cuts fast and is suited to rough work like paint removal and wood shaping, as mentioned earlier. For finer work it must be used with great skill and care.

The rigid disk sander is often mounted in place of the blade of a table saw. The sandpaper is stuck to the disk with a special "peelable" adhesive that permits abrasive removal and replacement quickly and easily. This type can be used for smoothing and for wood trimming, much as a planing machine might be used.

The ball joint disk is also a rigid form. But the sandpaper disk is attached in the same manner as on the flexible disk, by a screw-flange at the center. The ball joint permits this disk to be used flat on the surface of the work, driven by a power drill. The centered screw flange is recessed so it does not contact the work surface, and the ball joint prevents the disk from digging in if the power drill is tilted during the operation. This is also a good finishing type of sander in the low price range.

All power sanders should be used with progressively finer grit sizes in finishing work, and must be kept moving over the work. If allowed to stand still while running they will cut a recess in the work surface. The technique of use, however, is quickly acquired. The best bet, practice on scrap material before tackling your first project.   G.D.

See also: POWER TOOLS; ANTIQUING; PAINTING.

⋀ To sand small blemish areas, wrap strip of abrasive paper around rubber eraser of pencil.

◀ To sand flat surfaces that may be slightly irregular (as a cupped board) use flannel or felt pad between abrasive paper and wood sanding block. This lets abrasive surface conform to that of wood being sanded.

How to Plan Your Home Additions

Refinish your basement, attic, garage or breezeway to add space, increase equity

▲ *One place to look for additional space in your home is at the top. Here, an attic has been refinished inexpensively into a cheerful bedroom for two children.*

Your home may be your castle, but are there also times when it does not live up to your expectations? Then perhaps it is time to provide the extra room you need for recreation, sleeping, craftwork, or to house a live-in relative.

The cost of converting an unfinished basement or attic, or even a breezeway or garage into extra living space need not be prohibitive. You can cut the total conversion cost to a third or even a quarter of a contracted job by doing much or all of the work yourself because, in most instances, labor costs far exceed the cost of materials.

Do-it-yourself home improvement is now easier than ever thanks to the availability of materials that eliminate much of the hard work that you would have had to do for a similar conversion only a decade ago. Examples of easy-to-use construction materials include self-stick floor tile, beautifully prefinished wall paneling of several varieties and almost endless designs, colors and textures, and attractive ceiling coverings that can be installed in a professional manner by anyone. So, it doesn't make much sense for the average homeowner to spend,

say, from fifteen hundred to two thousand dollars on a home improvement job that he can do in his spare time for perhaps five hundred dollars.

The secret of success really comes down to one thing: careful planning. Plan all major design features of the new room in detail before buying materials or starting work; shop thoroughly for the best construction materials for your purpose (should walls be of plywood, hardboard or gypsum board, for example); compare prices of competitive materials, but do not sacrifice quality for cheapness; buy lumber in standard sizes and in lengths that minimize waste; seek reliable information concerning proper installation of construction materials that are unfamiliar to you.

Evaluate the relative merits of finishing an attic or basement, or perhaps adding an extension onto your home. Each home, and

How to Plan Your Home Additions

the space requirements of the family that lives in it are to some degree unique; the type of space expansion that was ideal for your neighbor may be a poor choice for you. So study in detail the pros and cons of converting all possible areas in your home. You might be surprised to conclude that the area that initially seems least attractive is in fact the best place in the home for improvement.

Basement. To this day you can find people—including some architects—who turn thumbs down on basement improvements on the grounds that below-grade rooms are damp, dingy and especially depressing if there are no windows. This may have been true in the past, but a basement room that is properly finished, properly illuminated, and equipped with dehumidifying equipment if necessary can be as pleasant as any other room in the home. Also, it is one of the best places for relatively noisy activities —within reasonable limits of course. For example, you wouldn't want to work in a woodworking shop under a bedroom when someone is sleeping. On the other hand, if you are trying to sleep, would you prefer that your teenagers dance above or below you?

A typical basement does not exhibit the cold and hot seasonal temperature extremes that are normal for attic areas. Thus cooling and heating is easier and less expensive, and there is no need to buy insulating materals for a roof.

The very first dollars spent on basement improvement can make the area more usable. For example, just by laying an inexpensive vinyl asbestos floor on the concrete sub-base you have an area that is much better for use as a play area. If money is on the short side, just paint concrete or block walls to add visual appeal at lowest possible cost.

Before starting more extensive improvements, take a critical look at your basement stairs. If they are too steep or flimsy, or if there is inadequate headroom (perhaps because of heating ducts), rebuild the stairway first. By adding a landing, and making the stairs turn a right angle, you may be able to provide extra headroom. Is there now a basement door leading to the yard? If not, consider adding one for convenience and safety. This outside entrance is especially important if you intend to put a woodworking shop in the basement. How else would you get large pieces of lumber into the shop? In fact, it may be impossible to get the 4-by-8 foot wall paneling for your recreation room into the basement until you add that outside entrance.

Wall paneling can be supported by a framework made of 2-by-3 or 2-by-4 studding, or you can save on lumber costs by using 1-by-2 or preferably 1-by-3 furring attached to the masonry wall. But what about electrical outlets? Clearly, these could not be set into walls where the space between the foundation and paneling is only one inch. This is a good example of the kind of oversight in initial planning that could lead to grief and be costly later on.

Basic electrical wiring is not difficult for any reasonably adept do-it-yourselfer who takes the trouble to consult readily available reference material. Just be sure that you understand local wiring regulations and that you have your work inspected by a town official before you bury it under paneling. By following the sensible rules established for your protection, you will have a safe place in which to live and play, and you can avoid unnecessary alterations. For example, if you install the ungrounded kind of outlet you have in your living room, in the basement, the electrical inspector will surely insist that you replace them with grounding type receptacles.

Analyze your basement area carefully during the initial planning stage to make sure that every cubic foot of usable space will be utilized to best advantage. For example, you probably have large sewer pipes running a couple of feet above the basement floor, along one or more walls. These should be hidden behind the new paneling, of course, but why run the paneling straight to the ceiling and thereby waste some excellent storage space? Instead, plan for cupboards or built-in bookcases above the pipes. Also, remember to use removable panel sections wherever there are clean-out plugs in the sewer piping.

Are you hard-pressed to find a good place to add that sauna you would like to have? Take a tip from one imaginative Finn who put his steam bath under a porch just off the kitchen by excavating and building a small room under the porch and adding a connecting door through the basement wall. A curtained-off corner of the basement recreation room served as a dressing room. Another advantage of placing the steam bath *outside* of the main house area is that it can be aired out easily to keep excessive moisture out of the house.

No basement improvements should be attempted if there is any problem whatever with excessive moisture or actual water leakage into the basement. Correct such faults before the remodeling begins and, to make sure all is well, wait until after a prolonged rainy spell before starting on major basement improvements. It can be heartbreaking to see water seeping under the new paneling you have so carefully installed. If complete waterproofing of the basement just isn't feasible at reasonable cost, you might be wiser to look for extra room in some other part of the house.

Attic. Finishing an attic is no more difficult than improving the basement unless dormers must be added to obtain more light, ventilation and/or headroom. But even the construction of a new dormer can be handled by a reasonably competent do-it-yourselfer. Small gable ("doghouse") dormers are useful mainly to provide light and ventilation; a larger shed dormer is

Not a window in sight, but refinished basement is still attractive. Note space-saving spiral staircase at right. One caution: don't decide to finish your basement until you are sure it is not incurably damp.

How to Plan Your Home Additions

used where extra headroom is required. You will also probably find that it is cheaper to build a shed dormer than to construct two or three doghouse dormers. Often, the original roof can be kept in place until the dormer is largely completed. Another possibility is raising a portion of the original roof to form the roof of a shed dormer; this is not as difficult or costly as one might think, but it is not the kind of job a do-it-yourselfer should attempt single handed.

It is especially important to provide sufficient headroom at the top of the attic stairs. If headroom cannot be achieved by adding a dormer, it may be possible to relocate the stairway, or to install a stairway that emerges where there is more headroom. For example, a prefabricated metal spiral stairway may be the ideal solution. And don't overlook the possibility of build-

▲ *Building an actual extension is the most costly way of increasing usable space. Improving existing space—attic, basement, garage or breezeway—is cheaper.*

ing a new stairway *outside* of the existing house structure. This could be especially convenient if the lower end of the stairway can lead to an outside door as well as to the lower floor of the house.

If the attic area is to be used for relatively noisy activities during evening hours, consider adding sound insulation to the floor. At least plan on using a thick carpet with a resilient pad underneath. If such wall-to-wall carpeting is to be used, do not waste money installing a fine hardwood floor that will never be seen.

A bathroom in the attic area is desirable, especially if the area is to be used for sleeping or for accommodating overnight guests. Try to locate the bathroom over an existing bathroom on the lower level to keep plumbing costs down.

Do not stint on insulation in the attic ceiling and walls. Use the best and heaviest insulation you can. You will then be more comfortable, and spend less on heating and air-conditioning expenses.

If the attic ceiling slants, try to make the knee walls at least four feet high to permit easy furniture placement. Don't overlook the possibility of adding storage drawers that slide through the walls into the unused portions of the attic, near the eaves. But, box in the drawer areas and insulate thoroughly. Other left-over areas of the attic, even if only high enough to be crawl spaces, should be made accessible for storage of items that are not used frequently.

Provide plenty of electrical outlets to power TV sets, radios, electric toys, and perhaps even space heaters in lieu of conventional hot water or hot air systems.

Garage conversion. If you don't mind leaving the car out in the open, or if you can provide a carport or other shelter elsewhere on your property, the existing garage can probably be converted into a very useful living area. The conversion may be quite easy, and cost less than you might think, because you already have a roof and three walls (the garage doors must be replaced by a fourth wall). The garage floor probably slopes toward the front, or toward a central water drain, and this will have to be leveled before you can add a tile floor. If headroom in the garage permits, it may be preferable to install a wooden floor at a somewhat higher level to bring the floor of the converted garage to the same level as the floors in the rest of the house. But be sure to scrub out all grease and oil from the original garage floor before covering it with a new floor, to eliminate all possibility of unwanted odors seeping into the room.

You may want to keep the garage ceiling where it is, or raise it higher, perhaps even form a cathedral ceiling. But do not start pulling out existing joists indiscriminately until you have found some other way to hold the garage structure together. If there is good storage space above the garage ceiling, make it available by adding a spiral staircase, or perhaps a fold-down

BASEMENT FINISHING COSTS			
Item	Unit Cost	Quantity Needed	Cost
Vinyl floor tile	$1/sq. ft.	320 sq. ft.	$320
Wall paneling	$16 each	18 panels	288
2-by-4 framing (walls)	24¢/foot	576 ft.	138
Acoustic ceiling tile	50¢/sq. ft.	320 sq. ft.	160
1-by-2 framing (ceiling)	10¢/ft	340 ft.	34
			$940

The basic cost of finishing a 16-by-20 foot basement area was around $940 in terms of early 1982 prices for medium quality floor tile, wall paneling and ceiling tile. To the estimated $940 add the cost of such incidentals as nails, adhesive to apply wall paneling, staples for ceiling tile, and purchase or rental of stapler. Also add expenditures for electrical wiring, fixtures, possibly professional service to connect the new wiring to the existing system. If you hire professional contractors to do the whole job, expect a total cost that is three to four times as much as the materials cost shown here.

How to Plan Your Home Additions

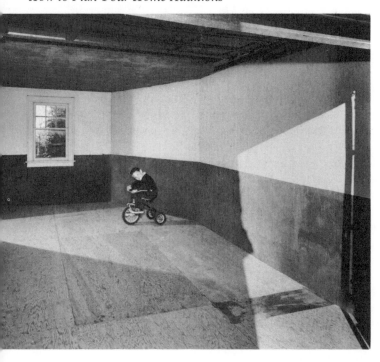

◄ *An attached garage is often a good prospect for refinishing to add living space to a house. Here, refinishing is under way, with new subflooring in place over the old garage floor.*

▼ *Use of prefinished wood paneling is one way to cut costs of home improvement. Here paneling is being installed in a new addition to a house.*

staircase. The attic, even if small, is an ideal place in which to store sporting equipment, games, or lumber if you make the garage into a shop.

If the garage door leading into the interior of the house now connects with the kitchen, it might be preferable to relocate it so that traffic can flow into and through a family room, living room or hallway. But before you start tearing out walls to create doorways, make certain that the walls do not contain water or heating system pipes that would be hard to relocate.

Plan new electrical wiring to suit the power requirements of the kind of room you are planning. Conventional wiring is adequate for a recreation room or den. But you should install heavier wiring, and several separate branch circuits, if the area is to be used for a shop containing such power tools as circular or radial arm saws, sanding machines, drill press.

The kind of paneling you use on the walls depends on how the room is to be used. A rumpus room where the kids will bang around should have plastic coated walls that are resistant to impact and easy to clean. Less rugged paneling can be used in a sitting room, or where no violent play is anticipated. For a shop or studio, consider using perforated hardboard which will make the hanging of tools or paintings a joy.

If the garage wall is of conventional wood construction, new paneling can be installed on the existing studding quickly and easily. If you have concrete walls, you will first have to add furring. Remember that thin, 1-by-3 furring can save you money but you would have to run new electrical wiring on top of the new paneling.

Porches and breezeways. If the garage you are converting to new uses is connected to the house by means of a breezeway, you should close in the breezeway as well so that getting to the new room will not entail dashing across a cold, windswept no-man's land.

Even if you leave the garage untouched, conversion of the breezeway into an all-seasons living area may be desirable. How useful this area would be for your needs depends on the size of the breezeway as is, or after expansion. Small or large, be sure that it is made just as weatherproof as the remainder of the house. Do not stint on insulation, and use double-glazed windows and sliding glass doors. Don't overlook the probable need of a radiator or two. If extending the conventional house heating system to this area is too complicated or costly, consider installing electrical heating units into the breezeway walls.

An open porch can also be converted into a closed-in room for year-around use provided it is at least nine feet in its shorter dimension, and if it has—or can be made to have—direct access to the kitchen, dining room, family room or hallway. If your main reason for doubting the wisdom of closing in the porch is that you would miss the cooling breezes during the summertime, just plan your renovation to include large screenable windows.

New wing. Suppose your basement is too wet for finishing or you have no basement, the attic has insufficient headroom, there is no porch or breezeway, and you can't bear the thought of evicting the family bus—then what? Your only recourse is to add a new extension to the house. This is bound to be the most costly way to solve your space problem because you must pay for new exterior as well as interior walls, insulation, and a supporting foundation. But if you do all or most of the work yourself, the cost may not be at all prohibitive.

You face at least two new planning problems if you decide to add an extension to your home. First, you must be sure that you have enough space on your lot, so that the addition does not violate set-back-requirements, and you must obtain approval of your building plan from the local building department. Secondly, unlike home improvements made inside your existing building, the new addition will be visible to neighbors. Be sure that the addition blends well with the existing structure and that it does not convert your home into an eye-sore that your neighbors will resent. If you have doubts about the visual aspects of the planned addition, consult an architect, or at least an experienced builder. And it wouldn't hurt to show your plans to your nearest neighbors to get their reaction, provided you can take honest criticism without feeling offended. Remember, you won't enjoy your new living space to the fullest extent if you see neighbors scowling across the backyard fence.   J.H.

See also: ATTIC; BASEMENTS; BATHROOMS; BREEZEWAYS; DORMERS; ELECTRICITY; GARAGE; HOME IMPROVEMENT; PAINTING, HOUSE; PANELS; ROOFS; WALL COVERINGS; WALLBOARD.

All about Adhesives

For decorating a window shade, repairing a camera or building a model boat, there's an adhesive that will do the job

Match a modern adhesive to the job and you can bond almost any material. Often the joint will be solid and waterproof in five minutes or less with a strength running to tons per square inch.

One versatile acrylic adhesive, for example, has been applied with a toothpick to mend a broken camera control and smeared on with a brush to bond an aluminum patch to the cracked iron hub of an earth moving machine.

There are epoxy glues that harden almost as fast on almost as many materials. One kind of epoxy holds heart pacers together. And, there are resocinol resin glues that bond boats together without nails, screws, or other metal fastening, so ruggedly that even after 20 years they have no leaks and require no caulking. And, there are completely flexible multi-resin adhesives that turn to rubber in minutes with such strength you can patch your work pants, your sail or your convertible top with greater strength than stitching. And there are less spectacular glues for everyday jobs. Some are so simple to use you just squeeze them on to a joint, stick the parts together and forget it. No clamps, no fuss.

Large hardware stores stock most of the modern glues. The remainder are available through marine suppliers or directly from the manufacturer. To pick the right one for the job at hand you need only the basic facts. For these, let the following data serve as your guide.

Acrylic resin adhesive. The fastest setting adhesive generally available. Based on the same formula used in high strength white dental fillings (you'll recognize the aroma) it sets in as little as five minutes to a strength of three tons per square inch. It is a two-part type (liquid and powder) with setting time varying from 5 to 20 minutes, according to the mixing proportions of the two components. A stiff mix gives short setting time, as wet mix longer setting time. It bonds to most materials including wood, metal, and ceramics. It is completely waterproof and widely used in marine repair work. It is also well suited to many types of delicate repair work, as on cameras, record players, etc. Clamping is no problem because parts can be hand-held while the adhesive sets. Sold in two-container packages consisting of two cans, or can and plastic jar combination.

Aliphatic resin glue. A leading furniture glue, this is a one-part beige liquid type that dries clear. It can also be colored with water soluble dyes to match the wood finish to be used. It is unaffected by most common finishes. Tackiness is similar to old style hot animal glues, making it possible to stick gluing blocks in furniture frame corners without clamping. Where clamps are required, glue is usually firm enough for clamp removal in about an hour. Allow overnight for complete set. It is moisture-resistant, but not waterproof. It is sold in squeeze bottles.

Buna-N adhesive. Originally developed for aircraft use, this is a one-part, thick beige liquid that will bond almost any material with a completely flexible and waterproof bond. It can bond fabric to metal or wood, metal to glass, even to bond patches to work clothes with greater strength than stitching.

Joints are usually pressed together while the applied adhesive is still wet.

In fabric-to-fabric bonding the dried adhesive-coated surfaces may be placed together and bonded by heating from the outside of one fabric piece, as with a flatiron. Sold in tubes and cans.

Casein glue. A strong, inexpensive adhesive with good moisture resistance (not waterproof) and gap-filling qualities that are useful in woodworking. It is a cream colored powder that must be mixed with water for use. It stiffens shortly after mixing, then becomes creamy on re-stirring. Follow the manufacturer's instructions carefully, and *do not* add water at the pre-stiffened stage. No longer widely available, it is stocked by cabinetmakers' supply houses and large hardware suppliers under various brand names.

Cellulose nitrate cement. Often called household cement or model airplane cement, this is a one-part water resistant adhesive, usually clear. (Some forms are tinted to make coated areas visible during work.) Dries firm enough for gentle assembly handling in unstressed work after an hour or two, for regular handling, overnight. It is sold largely in tubes.

Contact cement. Developed for bonding plastic laminates to plywood counters, and similar applications. Available in very quick-drying (flammable) types and in non-flammable form. It is applied to both meeting surfaces to be bonded, and

⋏Broken nib of camera exposure guide (at pencil tip) was permanently reattached with acrylic adhesive. The job took about 10 minutes. The same adhesive was used to bond an aluminum patch over the cracked cast iron hub of an earth moving machine.➤

All about Adhesives

allowed to dry completely. A wrapping paper "slip sheet" is then placed between the coated surfaces so they can be aligned without touching each other. The sheet is slipped out while the parts are held in alignment, permitting the cement-coated surfaces to come into contact. Permanent bond is made instantly on contact. A rubber roller is used to assure firm, full-area contact and work any trapped air bubbles outward to escape at edges. Contact cement is widely available through hardware stores under many brand names, mainly in cans, but occasionally in tubes.

Epoxy glue. A two-part adhesive comprising a liquid resin and liquid hardener. Available in both clear and opaque types, this is a completely waterproof adhesive that bonds most materials. The usual types set firm overnight and continue to increase in strength for a week or more. They are often used in marine fiberglassing and hull repairs. Quick-setting types are available with hardening times as short as 10 minutes. As formulas vary widely, follow the manufacturer's instructions in mixing and using any epoxy. In buying, specify the characteristics you require, clear, etc. Sold by hardware and marine suppliers under many brand names.

Epoxy, water-phase type. Relatively new to the retail market, this type may be used either as a coating or as an adhesive, and, prior to setting, can be washed from brushes and tools with water. Once hard, it is completely waterproof. It is a two-part type. Two liquid components are mixed in equal proportions for use. Complete setting time is around eight hours. Unmixed left-

▲ *For two-part glues like resorcinol resin twin measuring cups and twin measuring spoons are a must, so no trace of hardener can accidentally get into the resin remaining in the original can. Paint one spoon handle white, the other black, and use dark one for dark glue component, light one for light component.*

▲ *For small job gluing, as with acrylics, keep medicine dropper rubber-banded to can of liquid component. Use flat stick to portion out powder, and break off fresh section of stick for each use. For small-quantity mixing use screw-off pop bottle caps, after removing plastic gasket. For slightly larger batches, use aluminum cookie cups.*

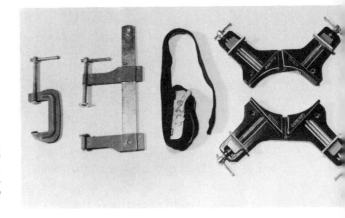

▶ *Clamps for most jobs. C-clamp at left is made in many sizes. Bar clamp next to it serves same purpose, but extends quickly to bridge wide gap, locks automatically for screw tightening. Band clamp to right of it can be wrapped like a belt around irregular work and drawn tight by turning built-in ratchet with wrench or screwdriver. Miter clamp at right locks mitered work like picture frames.*

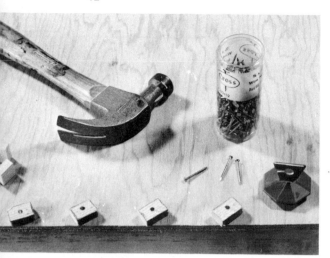

▲ *Nailing blocks can take the place of clamps where too many clamps would be required. Brads are driven through small wood blocks, tight, holding long glue line firmly.*

▲ *Nailing blocks are easily removed (with nails or brads) after glue has set. Here, nail puller has lifted one block and brad from the work.*

overs last indefinitely if containers are tightly closed. It is made in clear, white, and colored forms, and can be tinted with the same dry colors used in cement work.

It can also be mixed with portland cement (follow instructions on the adhesive containers) to make a high strength bonding filler for masonry repairs and similar jobs. The adhesive cement mix has a much shorter setting time than the adhesive alone, so plan to work accordingly. Ideal for fiberglassing seams on plywood porches and decks, it also is used with mineral granules for non-skid surface around swimming pools. It is sold in twin cans.

Hide Glue. This is available mainly in liquid form through hardware stores, though some cabinetmakers' supply houses still stock the traditional flake and sheet form. The latter forms must be water-soaked, then heated for use. Known as "hot glue," this type must be applied to joints and clamped before cooling. In the common liquid form it is used like any other one-part liquid glue. Usually it will harden overnight into a bond that is stronger than wood, but it is not very moisture resistant.

Hot-melt resin glues. Polyethylene-base types are used in electric glue gun cartridges. They bond to most materials, and are waterproof and moderately flexible. Because they harden by cooling, they are in the fast-setting class and require quick assembly of the parts to be glued. They are sold in cartridge form to fit specific glue guns.

Multi-resin hot melt glue is also available for special uses without a glue gun. These usually are sold in foil trays, and are melted on a heating device, such as a hot plate. Types like "Hot Grip" are used for bonding to plastics that will not accept other adhesives, such as polyethylene and polypropylene.

Neoprene-base adhesives. These are the types widely used in caulking guns to mount wall paneling. Now, combination resin forms are also used in house frame construction to bond sheathing to framing.

Characteristics vary with the brand, and the manufacturer's instructions should be followed carefully.

Polyester resin glue. Best known as a boat fiberglassing adhesive, this type is also a strong, quick-setting, waterproof wood glue that can be used clear or colored with pigments sold for the purpose. It is a two-part type. A liquid resin and a liquid catalyst are mixed just before use. Typically, a specified number of drops of catalyst from a small squeeze bottle are stirred into a quart or pint can of the resin. A portion of the resin may be poured off and mixed with a corresponding portion of catalyst. The amount of catalyst is important; an excess will harden the resin before it can be applied.

Temperature of the working area is also a factor because hardening time shortens as the working area temperature rises. Temperature-hardening time charts are available from suppliers for many resin brands. Do not apply a chart for one brand to another brand of resin; formulas vary widely.

Polyester resin glue is sold in cans, usually with plastic tube of catalyst in a plastic overcap, by boatyards, marine suppliers and large hardware outlets. Shelf life of unused resin varies with brand and storage conditions, so buy it fresh, as needed.

Polysulphide. Also known as Thiokol, this type is widely used as a marine caulking compound, though it is also a strong, completely waterproof adhesive with great flexibility and unusual vibration-damping qualities. The two-part form requires the mixing of two thick pastes. The one-part form sets by reaction with moisture in the air. When set, polysulphide is actually synthetic rubber, so mixed leftovers may be formed into gaskets, tires for toy wheels, etc. Molds with oiled surfaces may be used.

Polyvinyl acetate glue. This is the familiar one-part "white glue." It is easy to use and stronger than wood, but its strength is affected by high humidity and high temperature. It is a handy woodworking glue for joints that do not require the glue, alone, to sustain a prolonged load. (Most furniture joints are designed so the wood takes the load, the glue holds the joint together.) This glue should not be used on bare metal because of possible corrosive effect. Sold in squeeze bottles under various brand names.

▼ *Squeeze-out of glue along glue line tells you if you have even clamp pressure along glue line. Note that more glue has squeezed out at clamp locations. Use more clamps or clamp work between two heavy pieces of scrap wood to distribute clamping pressure evenly.*

▼ *How tight should clamps be? Make test joint with scrap wood. Tighten clamps. Then, unclamp, and open joint. If meeting surfaces show coating of glue, pressure was not excessive. If clamped too tight almost all glue will be squeezed out of joint, making weak bond.*

Resorcinol resin glue. This two-part (liquid and powder) glue is generally accepted as the best completely waterproof glue for wood. Originally developed for torpedo boat construction, it is stronger than wood, completely waterproof, (even in prolonged boiling) and unaffected by gasoline, oil, mild alkalis, mild acids, or common solvents. A working advantage: before hardening, it can be washed from brushes and tools with water.

Hardening time depends on temperature. Once components are thoroughly mixed according to manufacturer's instructions, the glue will cure in about 10 hours at 70 degrees, or in as little as 3½ hours at 90 degrees.

Mix proportions by volume are usually four measures of the liquid component to three measures of the powder. Very important: protect your eyes from both parts when mixing. And, before mixing, shake the closed can of powder thoroughly to "fluff" it. It tends to pack during storage, so volume measure is thrown off unless it is shaken up. Resorcinol resin glue is sold in twin cans by hardware stores and marine suppliers.

Rubber base adhesive. A one-part waterproof type that bonds to most materials, rubber base adhesive can be applied as a sealer even under water for emergency repairs. It should not be used where exposed to gasoline or oil, however, as both act on it as solvents. It is sold in tubes and cans by hardware stores.

Urea formaldehyde glue. Now usually called plastic resin glue, this is a one-part powder type that is mixed with water for use. It is stronger than wood, and highly water resistant but not quite waterproof. It is not a gap-filler type, however, and requires well fitted joints. Use this glue for general woodworking, especially where high humidity or high temperatures are likely, as it remains strong under both conditions. It is sold in cans under various trade names.

In woodworking, match the nature of the glue to the job. Thermoplastic adhesives can be softened by heat. Thermosetting ones can't. Thermoplastic glues (like white glue) shouldn't be used on joints where the glue alone must sustain a constant load, as in a simple lap joint. They are fine, however, in joints where the glue holds the joint together and the form of the joint takes the load, as where one part is notched into another.

For joints where the glue alone must take the load use a thermosetting type like plastic resin glue or resorcinol resin glue.

For plastics pick a glue that suits the particular material to be glued. Unless you're an expert, you can't tell the type of a plastic by looking at it. So select a glue (usually in a tube) that is labeled for use with plastics, often with a list printed on it. Try a small dab on a concealed part of the object to be bonded. After half a minute, wipe off the dab. If it leaves a shallow recess in the plastic, it has taken a "bite" and will usually do a good bonding job on it. This test works on thermoplastic

▼ *Use flexible spray adhesive to bond fabric to window shades. Spray adhesive on shade, apply fabric while adhesive is wet, spread smooth with hands, as shown.*

All about Adhesives 45

materials (a wide variety of plastics) but not on thermosetting types like Bakelite. For these, you need an adhesive that actually bonds to the material, as it can't bite into it by dissolving the surface. Try such adhesives as the epoxies, acrylics, and multi-resin-bond-anything types. Casein can also bond a wide range of materials.

Spray adhesives are made in many forms, and are usually flexible when set. Read the label on the container before you buy, to make certain the adhesive will bond the material you have in mind. Many are made for art work, as in bonding paper to backing board, but can be used for many other purposes, such as a non-flammable type used to bond cotton fabric to a paper window shade. The shade was sprayed, and the fabric smoothed onto it while the adhesive was still wet. Always follow the manufacturer's instructions. **G.D.**

⋏ *Hot-melt resin glue applied by glue gun bonds most materials, sets in seconds on cooling. Have parts ready for quick assembly before glue cools.*

See also: BOAT BUILDING; FURNITURE; BASEMENTS; BATHROOMS; PATCHING.

SELECTING THE RIGHT ADHESIVE		
Type of Adhesive	**Setting Time**	**Bonding Uses**
Cellulose (household or model airplane) cements	2-10 minutes	wood, metal, leather, paper, glass, ceramics
China/glass cements	2-5 minutes	china and glass
Cyanocrylate adhesives ("super glue")	10-30 seconds	solid, nonporous materials (metal, china, glass, jewelry, rubber, plastics, ceramics, leather)
Epoxy adhesives (epoxy resin and catalyst or hardener)	4-6 hours	glass, metal, concrete, porcelain, many plastics
Fabric-mending cements	24 hours	wool, cotton, canvas, leather, denim
Hot melt glues	60 seconds	porous materials
Paper adhesives (rubber cement, mucilage, library pastes)	————	paper, vinyl wallcovering; woodworking; household uses
Plastic mending cements	2-3 hours	flexible/rigid plastics (styrene, vinyl, acrylic, phenolic resins)
Plastic rubber cements (neoprene rubber paste)	2-3 hours	boot/rainwear leaks; seal/caulk wood, metal, canvas seams; insulate/weatherproof electrical connections, wires
Polyester adhesives	varied	fiberglass fabrics, stone work, marble
Polyvinyl chloride adhesives	10-30 minutes	porcelain, marble, metal, plastics
Rubber-base adhesives	————	nonporous materials (metals, masonry, glass, plastics, tiles)
Silicone adhesives	————	tub/shower areas; glass, ceramic, metal, plastics, wood, canvas, rubber

Servicing Your Car's Thermostatic Air Cleaner

Neglect of these vacuum and temperature controlled devices can lead to engine stalling and poor gas mileage

THE THERMOSTATICALLY-CONTROLLED air cleaner was originally conceived to improve cold engine operation, and is now part of the anti-air-pollution package, on Ford, GM and Chrysler products. (Chrysler uses the GM device.)

The Ford and GM units do the same thing (although in somewhat different ways). They duct intake air over the exhaust manifold to preheat it for better combustion when the engine is cold. They keep the intake air at a temperature of about 100 degrees F. until the engine warms up. Each has a vacuum override system that bypasses the duct and opens the regular air cleaner neck or snorkel on hard acceleration. When the engine warms up, all the air comes from the air cleaner neck or snorkel.

The Ford system has a thermostatic assembly that holds a valve in the air cleaner intake neck so that exhaust-manifold-heated air flows into and through the air filter. As the engine warms, heating the air in the engine compartment, the thermostatic assembly lengthens, and through linkage, pivots the valve to restrict (and finally close) the opening to the duct over the exhaust manifold. The valve also can be pivoted by a vacuum diaphragm device that is spring-loaded. When the throttle is floored, the manifold vacuum drops, and the spring-loaded device pushes on another link to pivot the valve. But the basic action is the same in both situations: the valve closes against the exhaust manifold duct and opens the air cleaner intake neck or snorkel.

Except for this vacuum override, the pivoting of the valve is gradual, and in the middle of engine warmup, the air that goes into the carburetor is a mixture of preheated air from the exhaust manifold cut and colder air entering through the air cleaner intake neck or snorkel.

To check the system, start with the engine cold and off, and an air temperature of no more than 85-95 degrees F. The air cleaner intake neck or snorkel should be closed off by the valve. If it isn't closed, the linkage is binding or the thermostatic unit is defective.

As the engine warms up, the valve should move, closing off the duct for the exhaust manifold preheated air. If it doesn't, the thermostat is defective, the linkage is binding or the vacuum override is defective. The simplest procedure is to check the linkage first, then the vacuum device, and if they are good replace the thermostatic assembly.

Before the engine fully warms up, open the throttle. This will cause manifold vacuum to drop, and the spring in the vacuum device should force the valve to move and

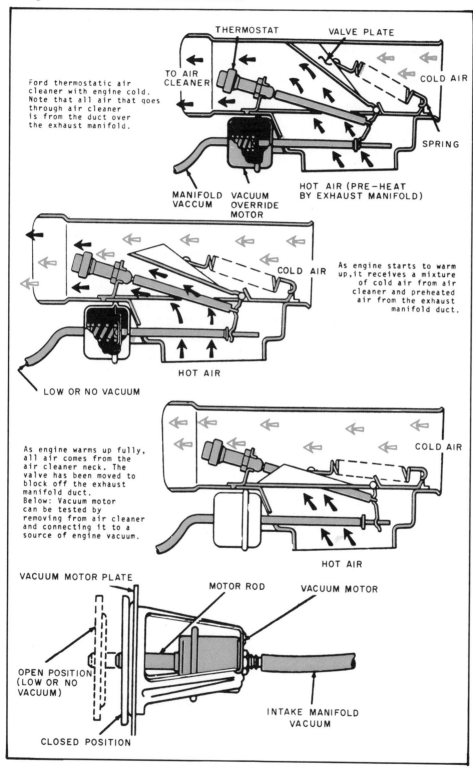

Ford thermostatic air cleaner with engine cold. Note that all air that goes through air cleaner is from the duct over the exhaust manifold.

THERMOSTAT   VALVE PLATE

TO AIR CLEANER   COLD AIR

SPRING

MANIFOLD VACCUM   VACUUM OVERRIDE MOTOR

HOT AIR (PRE-HEAT BY EXHAUST MANIFOLD)

As engine starts to warm up, it receives a mixture of cold air from air cleaner and preheated air from the exhaust manifold duct.

COLD AIR

HOT AIR

LOW OR NO VACUUM

As engine warms up fully, all air comes from the air cleaner neck. The valve has been moved to block off the exhaust manifold duct.
Below: Vacuum motor can be tested by removing from air cleaner and connecting it to a source of engine vacuum.

COLD AIR

HOT AIR

VACUUM MOTOR PLATE   MOTOR ROD   VACUUM MOTOR

OPEN POSITION (LOW OR NO VACUUM)

INTAKE MANIFOLD VACUUM

CLOSED POSITION

open the air cleaner intake neck. If it doesn't, check for 15 inches of vacuum at the hose connection to the vacuum device (using an inexpensive vacuum-fuel pressure gauge, available at auto supply stores).

Low or no vacuum indicates a bad hose or connection. If vacuum is good, check the vacuum device. Remove the vacuum device from the air cleaner and connect it to a source of vacuum on the engine. (There should be one at the carburetor base, such as the PCV hose neck.) With vacuum applied, the device's link should be held against the entire assembly. Disconnect the hose and it should spring outward about a half inch. The vacuum device (called a "motor" by Ford) is not normally rebuildable. Replace it if it is defective.

When the engine is fully warm, the valve should close off the exhaust manifold duct and open the air cleaner intake neck. Just look into the air cleaner neck and see if it is open. Note: if the vacuum device operates the linkage and moves the plate, the linkage obviously is good. If a good vacuum device fails to move the linkage, it is binding. Free up linkage by working in a good solvent. (The aerosol type used for carburetor linkage is ideal for this purpose.) If the linkage is free and the vacuum device works outside the air cleaner, any defect in the system can be traced to the thermostatic unit.

The GM system, like the Ford, uses a pivoting valve in the air cleaner intake neck and the valve is connected by linkage to a vacuum diaphragm device. But here the similarity ends. The GM system incorporates a temperature sensor inside the air cleaner housing. When the engine is off, a spring inside the vacuum diaphragm device holds the valve against the exhaust manifold air duct. When the engine is started cold, vacuum passes through the sensor into the vacuum diaphragm device, open-

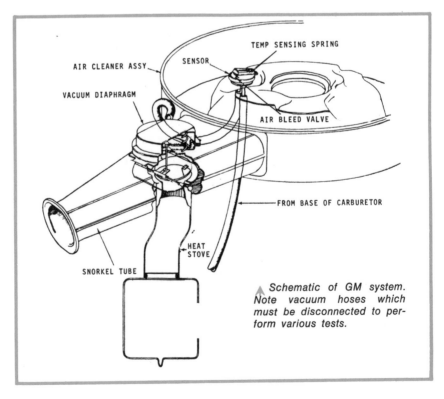

▲ *Schematic of GM system. Note vacuum hoses which must be disconnected to perform various tests.*

ing the exhaust manifold air duct and closing off the air cleaner intake neck. As the sensor heats up, it bleeds off vacuum to the atmosphere, and the pressure of the spring against the diaphragm inside the vacuum device moves the valve to close the exhaust manifold air duct.

On GM cars with double-snorkel air cleaners and four-barrel carburetor, only one snorkel has the temperature-sensitive arrangement and one duct over the exhaust manifold. The other has a vacuum diaphragm controlled valve and it closes off the snorkel. When the throttle is opened, manifold vacuum drops and a diaphragm spring forces open the valve to admit additional air for higher performance. The second snorkel works this way whether the engine is hot, cold or in-between.

To check the GM system, proceed as follows: With the engine cold and not running, the air cleaner intake neck should be open. Start the engine and one valve should close. As the engine warms up, that valve should move and cover the exhaust manifold air duct (which you will not be able to see), opening the air cleaner intake neck (which you will be able to see).

Before the engine fully warms, open the throttle, which will cause manifold vacuum to drop. The thermostatically-controlled valve should open (so should the other snorkel's valve on double-snorkel setups).

If the valve is in the wrong position with the engine off, the cause is binding linkage or a defective spring in the vacuum device. If the valve fails to close the air cleaner intake neck when the cold engine is started, check for at least eight inches of vacuum at the end of the hose that connects the carburetor base or intake manifold to the sensor in the air cleaner. Less than this amount indicates a defective hose or connection.

If vacuum is good at the sensor, check it at the vacuum device hose connection. If it is low, check the hose, and if this is good, replace the sensor. Adequate

▲ Top: *Pivoting valve of GM system. Valve should be open (as shown) when engine is warm and running. When engine is cold, valve should close air cleaner snorkel. Above: Air cleaner element removed. Vacuum sensor is at upper left, near center depression in air cleaner base.*

vacuum at this hose, combined with failure of the valve to move when the engine is started, indicates a leaking vacuum diaphragm device. Reconnect the hose and pinch it firmly (or kink it) to trap vacuum. The valve in the air cleaner neck should close off with the vacuum applied. If the valve doesn't do this, or if the valve starts to open with the hose firmly pinched or kinked, a leaking diaphragm is likely. This test is excellent as a general check of the vacuum device, as it will spot a minor leak before it becomes major.

Removing vacuum sensor from GM system (on Chrysler products).

Closeup of vacuum diaphragm assembly from Chrysler products.

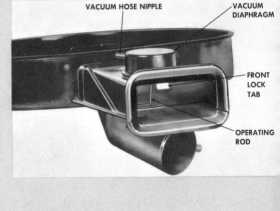

Removing vacuum diaphragm from Chrysler products.

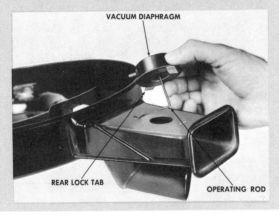

Checking the snorkel valve that responds only to vacuum changes is simple. With the engine idling, the snokel should be closed off by the valve. Open the throttle (causing manifold vacuum to drop) and the valve should swing open. If you have an engine with a two-barrel carburetor and a double-snorkel air cleaner, one snorkel is strictly jazz. It's blocked off by a plate and that plate won't move.

There are all sorts of special thermome-ters and time-consuming techniques for checking thermostatic air cleaners to see if they are right within specifications. But the specifications are reasonably wide, and if the unit is out of specifications, the condition will probably show up with the engine dying immediately after starting, carburetor icing or poor gas mileage that can't be traced to something else.   P.W.

See also: ANTI-POLLUTION; ENGINES; FILTERS; HEAT RISER, AUTO.

What You Should Know about Air Conditioners

Here's how to narrow down a field of more than 3,000 types, models and sizes to the unit that meets your requirements

I F YOU ARE IN THE MARKET for an air conditioner, make your purchase as an informed consumer. Resist any impulse to dash out on a Saturday morning and "pick up" any air conditioner that an eager salesman assures you will be just right for your medium-sized bedroom. It might be just right—but only through sheer chance. But, why depend on luck when choosing wisely is easy, and you stand to save a considerable amount of money on both the initial investment and on year-by-year operating expenses.

About 55 different companies now manufacture a total of almost 3,000 models of room air conditioners in the U.S. The appliances include window, through-the-wall and combination cooler-heater models. The cooling capacities range all the way from about 4,000 BTU/hour to about 34,000 BTUs. There's nothing mysterious about the term BTU which is just an abbreviation for British thermal unit, a standard unit used to measure heat quantities. In this case the BTU/hour is the amount of heat that a

given air conditioner can remove from the surrounding air in one hour. Thus a 10,000 BTU unit can remove twice as much heat from the air, in any given time, as a 5,000 BTU model. But as we shall see, there is a little more to picking the right air conditioner than deciding how many BTUs your unit should be able to handle. Not all 10,000 BTU units, even if superficially identical, are necessarily equally good.

Since the appliance uses electricity, your first job is to decide what type and size of air conditioner your existing power line can handle. House convenience outlets are usually rated at 115 volts and 15 amperes. If you want to avoid adding new wiring to your home, see if a 4,000 to 9,900 BTU/ hr. unit drawing a maximum of 7.5 amperes will do the job (we will discuss later how to make such judgments). If it will, you can just plug it into the handiest wall outlet and be done with it. If you decide to buy a unit that draws as much as 12 amperes (typical 7,000 to 14,000 units), use a 115-

volt, 15-ampere circuit, but make sure that no other electrical appliance is used on the same branch circuit at the same time. If you need still more cooling power (anywhere from 8,000 to 34,000 BTU), you will have to install a 230/208 volt circuit wired and fused for 15, 20, 30 or perhaps even 50 amperes depending on the current draw of the appliance you select. This circuit, independently fused, should supply power only to the air conditioner.

Types of systems. There are several types of air conditioning equipment, and each has special characteristics that make it suitable for specific applications. Refer to the *Air Conditioning Decision Guide* to determine what types probably would suit your needs, but remember that these are generalizations.

Central (whole house) air conditioning system. This type of system consists of an evaporator (cooling) coil, condenser coil (usually located outside the building), compressor, circulating refrigerant, two fans or blowers, and usually a humidity control and one or more air filters.

Warm, moist air, from inside the house is drawn by a fan blower through a filter and passes over cooling coils which absorb the heat. The heat is carried away by a refrigerant in tubes running to the outdoor condensing unit where the heat is transferred to the atmosphere by a fan in the condensing unit. The cooling coil also re-

AIR CONDITIONING DECISION GUIDE

The type of building you (1) already own or rent or (2) plan to build or rent in the future should be considered when you attempt to choose the basic type of air conditioning system that would probably be most economical and otherwise best suited for your needs. This two-choice decision guide will help you steer toward a good decision:

Type of Residence	First Consideration	Second Consideration
Planned New Construction:		
Single family home	Central A/C system	
Duplex	Two Central A/C systems	Zone systems
Mobile home	Self-contained or split system Central A/C	Mobile home room A/C
Add-on rooms for existing home	Air zone heating/cooling system	Room A/C unit
Vacation home	Heat pump units	Room A/C units
Existing Construction:		
Own single family home with warm air heating (ducts)	Central A/C system	
Own single family home with hot water heating (no ducts)	Room A/C units	
Own duplex apartment house with warm air heating (ducts)	Central A/C system	
Own duplex apartment house with hot water or individual heating systems	Air zonal cooling units	Room A/C units
Rent single family home	Room A/C units	Air zone system
Rent apartment	Room A/C units	
Own mobile home	Self-contained mobile home unit	

moves excessive moisture from the room air to effect dehumidification. The cooled and dehumidified air is circulated throughout the house through ductwork.

If your home has a heating system with ducts running to all parts of the house, the central air conditioning system can make use of the existing ducts *unless* (1) the furnace is in very cramped quarters and there is not enough room for the new equipment, (2) the ductwork goes only to a few central locations, or (3) the house is only partially heated or inadequately heated by a central heating system.

You can save money, use space more efficiently, and have a single control if you install a combination air conditioning and central heating system using common ductwork in a new house before construction is completed. But there are conditions wherein central air conditioning is not feasible: (1) the home is in a warm climate where central heating is unnecessary, (2) the building is used only occasionally in cold weather (vacation retreat, for example), (3) the building is occupied by more than one family and separate heating-cooling systems for each are desirable, (4) the building will frequently have unoccupied areas or rooms

▲ *Central air conditioning for single family dwellings often is designed so that much of the mechanism is outside the house, as in this unit. Cooling coils are inside, where air blown over them is carried to various rooms by ducts.*

▼ *Central air conditioning can be installed in various ways. At top left, cooling coils are in existing hot-air ducts. Where there is no hot-air heating system, ducts can be installed in attic (top right) or beneath floor (bottom).*

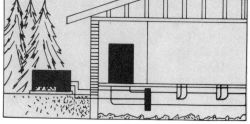

and (5) special heating or structural considerations call for use of ductless hot water heating.

Central combination systems. In a new structure, any one of four different types of central air conditioning can be installed, separately or in conjunction with the heating system: (1) basement installation having the evaporator coil and air distributor fan inside and the condenser outside of the building, (2) ground level installation in which the system is located in a closet or utility room (condenser outside), (3) attic installation with ductwork running to all parts of the building and (4) roof mount installation where all of the cooling equipment is on the roof (not suitable for combination heating-cooling systems).

Zonal combination heating-cooling systems. Zone heating and cooling units are efficient, uncomplicated, relatively low in cost and eliminate the need of ductwork and heavy conduit wiring. The units consist of single packages containing complete air conditioning equipment plus an electric heating coil grid. A common fan disperses the warm or cool air. These are especially suitable in such places as add-on rooms where individual control of temperature and humidity are desirable. They can be left off when the room is unoccupied. Installation is in an opening cut into an outside wall near where a 230-volt outlet is available.

Room window units. These units are very popular because they can be added to existing homes very quickly and easily, just by mounting into a window opening. If you are shopping for this type of air conditioner, be especially careful to buy good equipment that meets your needs best. A room air conditioner should have an energy efficiency rating (EER) of eight or more to assure minimum electricity costs and maximum efficiency.

Room air conditioners are made to operate off 115-volt or 208/230-volt power lines. If you have an outlet providing the higher voltage near the window where the air conditioner is to be installed, you can use a unit having greater cooling capacity than is provided by most 115-volt jobs (top limit about 14,000 BTU/hr. capacity). Just bear in mind that a *room* air conditioner is just that—a room conditioner—so don't expect it to cool your entire house or apartment. Even if it were large enough in terms of BTU capacity, you would have big problems keeping air circulating from room to room to maintain an even coolness throughout your habitat.

The operating cost (cost of electricity) of a room air conditioner can range from about $15 per year for a 4,000 BTU/hour unit to more than $148 per year for a 35,000 BTU/hour unit, assuming an operating period of 1,440 hours and an average kilowatt hour cost of two cents for electrical power. You will keep the operating cost on the low side if you buy a unit of the proper size with the highest efficiency rating (EER), consistent with other factors that must influence your purchase decision.

Insist that the dealer demonstrate your tentative choice of air conditioner so that you can evaluate the noise level, at both high and low speeds. Remember that the unit may sound noisier in your home in the quiet of the night than it does in a store having a much higher background noise level. If you find heavy insulation in the air chamber behind the air discharge grille, you have evidence that the manufacturer has paid some attention to sound control.

The features found on different models and brands of air conditioners are not all the same. Look for and consider the desirability of the following: exhaust control for removal of smoky or stale air from the room; vent setting to bring outside fresh air into the room quickly; thermostat control plus automatic fan shut-off control so that the fan stops when the room air is as cool as you want it; air directors that help control air flow into the room so as to avoid annoying drafts. Also be sure that the selected unit has both the UL (Underwriters Laboratories) seal of approval and the AHAM (Association of Home Appliance Manufacturers) certified seal. Also examine the name plate which shows the model number and rated capacity, the BTU rating and wattage.

Heat pumps. These are window air conditioning units that provide both heating and cooling. They are especially popular for use in vacation homes, and in permanent homes in warm climes where winters are very mild. In northern areas they can be used for supplemental heating in the winter and for efficient cooling in the summer.

Heat pumps can reverse operation and take warmth from the outside air and bring it into the room to be heated. Surprisingly, the heat pump will extract warmth from the atmosphere even when the temperature is quite low. Heat pumps look much like regular window air conditioners, and they are installed just as easily.

Through-the-wall air conditioners. These are merely variations of window-type heat pumps in that they are installed in openings cut into the walls, rather than in windows. The main advantage is that use of the window for ventilation, illumination and visibility is not impaired.

Mobile home air conditioners. The heating ductwork is too small and the furnace blower capacity too weak in a typical mobile home to permit efficient integration of an air conditioning unit. However, you can obtain a self-contained unit that fits neatly under the floor of the mobile home and connects to existing ductwork by means of flexible ducts. These units are especially good for small mobile homes having about 750 square feet of living space.

Another type of mobile home air conditioner, called a split system, consists of an evaporator unit which fits snugly under the floor, and a condensing unit outside, ad-jacent to the mobile home. This system is good for larger mobile homes. Whatever type you buy, be sure it operates very quietly so that you won't annoy neighbors and/or violate mobile park regulations.

Help your dealer to help you. To shop intelligently for air conditioning equipment, you need to prepare yourself with facts and figures that either you or your appliance dealer can use to calculate the capacity unit you need. If you just ask a dealer to recommend a good unit for a "small bedroom," or whatever, he may try to do so. But don't be surprised if the cooler turns out to be too weak or too powerful.

If you reason that you can't go wrong by purchasing a unit that is a little bigger than that suggested by the dealer, you may be buying *poorer* performance at higher cost. The reason: an oversize unit can be worse than one that is undersized because it will cool the air too quickly; it won't have time enough to *dehumidify* the air properly. Thus the room may feel cool, but uncomfortably "clammy." If the calculated optimum cooling capacity should figure out to, say, 10,000 BTU, and you have a choice of a 9,000 or 11,000 BTU unit because the exact capacity model is out of stock, take the lower-capacity job. The only exception: if you live in a very dry section of the country where excess humidity is never a problem.

Before you go shopping, prepare a list showing the following information about the room where you plan to install the unit: floor area, room height, type of wall and ceiling insulation, whether there is another room above the one to be cooled, total glass area in windows and doors in the room, the type of glass used in the doors and windows (thickness, and whether they are of double-glazed insulating type), the number of people who normally use the room (to account for added body heat), the compass direction the room faces, whether the room receives direct sunlight or is shaded, and a list showing the wattage ratings of all heat-producing electrical devices and appliances in the room (light bulbs, TV sets, stereo sound equipment and the like).

Using such pertinent information, your dealer should be able to make a reasonably accurate estimate of your cooling needs. If your appliance dealer obviously does not attempt to calculate the cooling load, taking into consideration a reasonable number of the factors listed above, seek a more conscientious salesman elsewhere.

Of course you should also have some advance idea of whether you want a room air conditioner that mounts in a window, in a hole cut in the wall, or one that also doubles as a room heater. If the appliance is to be set into a wall, determine whether the selected wall area is clear of such obstructions as heating ducts, plumbing or hard-to-move electrical wiring.

Just where you locate the air conditioner in a room can make a very big difference in how well it will perform. It should not be placed too close to the floor, too near an adjacent wall, or where an easy chair or sofa might obstruct air flow. If the air conditioner is placed where air circulation is hampered, the cooler thermostat may be fooled into "thinking" that the entire room is as cool as the stagnant air near the air conditioner, and it may cut off sooner than it should. This operating fault is called "short cycling."

Energy Efficiency Ratings (EER). On January 1, 1973, the Association of Home Appliance Manufacturers (AHAM) began providing specific comparable information concerning the efficiencies of nearly 3,000 room air conditioner models sold under various brand names—in the form of energy efficiency ratings (EER). The EER is calculated by dividing the BTU per hour of cooling by the watts of power used. Obviously a unit of the same "size" that gives the most cooling per watt will cost less to operate than one using more power for the

COOLING CAPACITY REQUIRED PER SQUARE FOOT OF FLOOR SPACE

APPROX. BTU CAPACITY REQUIRED	OCCUPIED ROOM			ATTIC			INSULATED FLATROOF		
	North or East	South	West	North or East	South	West	North or East	South	West
4,000	160	90	45	120	60	30	120	60	30
6,000	325	205	150	270	175	120	240	160	115
8,000	490	330	255	420	285	220	355	250	195
10,000	670	450	360	580	400	325	475	345	280
12,000	885	580	465	735	520	420	600	445	360
14,000	1200	720	580	900	640	525	730	540	445
16,000	—	880	690	1095	760	630	865	645	535
18,000	—	1090	820	—	885	745	1005	745	625
20,000	—	—	970	—	1030	855	1185	855	720
22,000	—	—	1185	—	1195	975	—	985	820
24,000	—	—	—	—	—	1120	—	1125	930
26,000	—	—	—	—	—	—	—	—	1060

NOTE: Based on an eight-foot ceiling height.

same amount of cooling. Energy efficiency ratings are published in the AHAM Directory of Certified Room Air Conditioners, which you should be able to see at any reputable air conditioner dealership.

To make comparison shopping easier, all appliance manufacturers have been required since May of 1980 to provide an "Energy-Guide" label that gives the EER of certain major appliances. The label also shows the yearly energy cost of operating an appliance, allowing consumers to compare it to the energy cost of competing models of similar size and features. When considered along with the purchase price, you can determine which appliance is less expensive to own and operate over the long run.

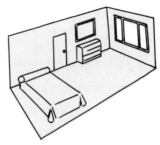

Height, width, and length of the area to be cooled

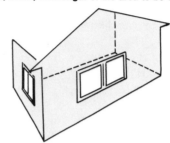

Number, sizes, and directions faced by windows

EnergyGuide labels are required on furnaces, refrigerators and refrigerator/freezers, freezers, water heaters, clothes washers, dishwashers, and room air conditioners. The EER, based on U.S. government standard tests, is printed in large numbers in the center of the label. The higher the number, the higher the relative efficiency of the appliance. There is also a range given, in the case of room air conditioners, for instance, for competing air conditioners of the same cooling capacity and a cost/use chart so you can calculate the energy cost of the appliance based on local electricity rates and expected hours of use.

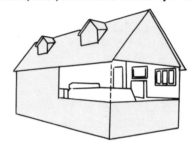

Location of space to be cooled within the building

Of course your final choice should not be dependent solely on picking the highest available efficiency rating. It is possible that another model or brand of equipment may have a slightly lower efficiency ratio and still represent a better buy because it is quieter, has features not found on the competing model, or because it obviously is made more carefully or of more durable materials.

On the other hand, it would be most unwise to ignore the efficiency ratings, even if you have an unshakeable loyalty to one particular brand of appliance. For exam-

Direction of the longest side of the space to be cooled

▲ *Factors to consider when determining required air conditioner capacity include dimensions of the area to be cooled, the amount of window area and the compass direction it faces, the location of the space within the building and the compass direction faced by the longest outside wall.*

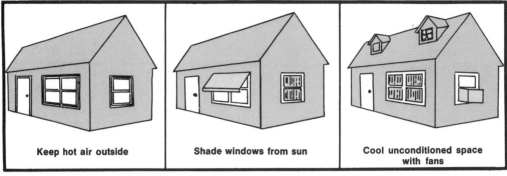

| Keep hot air outside | Shade windows from sun | Cool unconditioned space with fans |

▲ *Use these tips to reduce your air conditioner's work load. Keep hot air outside by keeping storm windows on and making sure drafty cracks are caulked. Shade windows from the sun with awnings on the outside and shades, drapes or blinds on the inside. Cool unconditioned space with fans.*

ple, one company offers two window model air conditioners rated at 14,000 BTU/hr. The 115-volt model has an EER rating of 10.2 whereas the 230/208-volt model is rated at only 6.0. Obviously, it will cost you a great deal more to operate the high-voltage model.

Even if a dealer does not have a copy of the AHAM directory listing the EER ratings for all air conditioners, you can easily make efficiency comparisons by checking the EER labels on every air conditioner the dealer displays. Above all, do *not* assume that air conditioners having the same cooling power in BTUs are pretty much the same. For example, one 10,000 BTU appliance listed in the AHAM directory draws 1,375 watts of power, so its efficiency ratio is 7.3; another 10,000 BTU appliance made by another manufacturer draws 1,850 watts to do the same amount of cooling work, so its efficiency ratio is a substantially lower 5.4. If you choose the second appliance, your electric bills will be larger than they need to be.

It is a good idea also to calculate the approximate cost of electricity used to operate various models. You need to know the cost per kilowatt of electricity in your area (ask your salesperson or local utility for this energy rate), and you need to make a rough estimate of the number of hours you would probably operate the appliance throughout the year. Then use the cost/use chart on the EnergyGuide labels, or get more exact amounts by doing the figuring yourself. For example, assume that electricity costs 2½ cents per kilowatt,

and that you will operate your air conditioner 1400 hours each year, on the average. First calculate the *base annual cost per watt* by multiplying the cost of electricity by the hours of use, and then divide the product by 1,000 to convert the cost per kilowatt to the cost per watt:

$$\frac{\$0.06 \times 750}{1000} = \$0.045$$

Armed with this basic figure, you can easily figure the approximate probable annual cost of operating any air conditioner, just by multiplying the base annual cost per watt (in this example, 0.045) by the wattage rating of the appliance in question. For example, consider the two 10,000 BTU units mentioned above. One draws 1,375 watts of power, so its operating cost per year would be about $61.87; the other unit draws 1,850 watts, so its operating cost would come to $83.25. The less efficient unit would, under these assumed circumstances, cost $21.38 more to operate each year.

When you consider that you could easily throw away that kind of money—not just once but every year your air conditioner is in use—through impulse buying, it's obvious that spending a little time figuring your real air conditioning needs is well worth the small effort involved.   J.H.

COOLING-LOAD ESTIMATE FORM

Heat Gain From	Quantity	Factors				Quantity X Factor

1. WINDOWS: Heat gain from sun.

		No shades*	Inside shades*	Outside awnings*	(Area x Factor)	
Facing northeast ......_____ sq. ft.		60	25	20		
Facing east ...._____ sq. ft.		80	40	25	_____	_____
Facing southeast ....._____ sq. ft.		75	30	20	_____	_____
Facing south ...._____ sq. ft.		75	35	20	_____	_____
Facing southwest ....._____ sq. ft.		110	45	30	_____	_____
Facing west ...._____ sq. ft.		150	65	45	_____	_____
Facing northwest ....._____ sq. ft.		120	50	35	_____	_____
Facing north ....,.._____ sq. ft.		0	0	0	_____	_____

These factors are for single glass only. For glass block, multiply the above factors by 0.5; for double glass or storm windows, multiply above factor by 0.8.

2. WINDOWS: Heat gain by conduction (total of all windows).

Single glass ...._____ sq. ft.		14	_____
Double glass or glass block ...._____ sq. ft.		7	_____

3. WALLS: (Based on linear feet.)

		Light construction	Heavy construction	
a. Outside walls				
North exposure ......_____ ft.		30	20	_____
Other than north exposure ...._____ ft.		60	30	_____
b. Inside walls (between conditioned and unconditioned spaces only) ...._____ ft.		30		_____

4. CEILING: (Use one only.)

Enter one figure only

a. Uninsulated with no space above ...._____ sq. ft.		19	_____
b. Insulation 1 inch or more, no space above ...._____ sq. ft.		8	_____
c. Uninsulated with attic space above ...._____ sq. ft.		12	_____
d. Insulated with attic space above ...._____ sq. ft.		5	_____
e. Occupied space above ...._____ sq. ft.		3	_____

5. FLOOR: (Disregard if floor is on ground or over basement.) ...._____ sq. ft.   3   _____

6. NUMBER OF PEOPLE: _____   600   _____

7. ELECTRICAL EQUIPMENT: ...._____ watts   3   _____

8. DOORS AND ARCHES OPEN TO UNCOOLED SPACE: ...._____ ft.   300   _____

9. SUBTOTAL: xxxxxxx   xxxxxxx   _____

10. TOTAL COOLING LOAD: Btu per hour to be used for selection of room air-conditioner(s) ......_____ (Item 9) X _____ (Factor from map) =

INSTRUCTIONS

The numbers of the following paragraphs refer to the correspondingly numbered item on the form:

1. Multiply the square feet of window area for each exposure by the applicable factor. The window area is the area of the wall opening in which the window is installed. For windows shaded by inside shades or Venetian blinds, use the factor for "Inside Shades." For windows shaded by outside awnings or by both outside awnings and inside shades (or Venetian blinds), use the factor for "Outside Awnings." "Single Glass" includes all types of single-thickness windows, and "Double Glass" includes sealed air-space types, storm windows, and glass block. Only one number should be entered in the right-hand column for item 1, and this number should represent *only the exposure with the largest load.*

2. Multiply the total square feet of *all* windows in the room by the applicable factor.

3a. Multiply the total length (linear feet) of all walls exposed to the outside by the applicable factor. Doors should be considered as being part of the wall. Outside walls facing due north should be calculated separately from walls facing other directions. Walls which are permanently shaded by adjacent structures should be considered as being "North Exposure." Do not consider trees and shrubbery as providing permanent shading. An uninsulated frame wall or a masonry wall 8 inches or less in thickness is considered "Light Construction." An insulated frame wall or a masonry wall over 8 inches in thickness is considered "Heavy Construction."

3b. Multiply the total length (linear feet) of all inside walls between the space to be conditioned and any unconditioned spaces by the given factor. Do not include inside walls which separate other air-conditioned rooms.

4. Multiply the total square feet of roof or ceiling area by the factor given for the type of construction most nearly describing the particular application. (Use one line only.)

5. Multiply the total square feet of floor area by the factor given. Disregard this item if the floor is directly on the ground or over a basement.

6. Multiply the number of people who normally occupy the space to be air-conditioned by the factor given. Use a minimum of 2 people.

7. Determine the total number of watts for lights and electrical equipment, except the air conditioner itself, that will be *in use* when the room air-conditioning is operating. Multiply the total wattage by the factor given.

8. Multiply the total width (linear feet) of any doors or arches which are continually open to an unconditioned space by the applicable factor. Where the width of the doors or arches is more than 5 feet, the actual load may exceed the calculated value. In such cases, both adjoining rooms should be considered as a single large room, and the room air-conditioner unit or units should be selected according to a calculation made on this new basis.

9. Total the loads estimated for the foregoing 8 items.

10. Multiply the sub-total obtained in Item 9 by the proper correction factor, selected from the map, for particular locality. The result is the total estimated design cooling load in Btu per hour. For best results a room air-conditioner unit or units having a cooling capacity rating as close as possible to the estimated load should be selected. In general, a greatly oversized unit which would operate intermittently will be much less satisfactory than one which is slightly undersized and which would operate more nearly continuously.

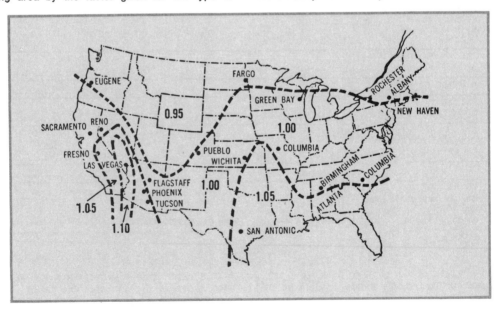

Seasonal Maintenance for Your Air Conditioner

Get this job done in the spring for dependable summer-long operation

▲ *Room air conditioners need seasonal check-up to keep them trouble-free. A little attention beforehand will avoid costly breakdowns. First step is to lift off the front cover, held by spring clips.*

TAKE A LOOK at your air conditioner before the hot weather strikes. Just a few maintenance details may be all it needs to get it into shape for dependable performance all season.

Two routine chores, often overlooked, are quickly gotten out of the way. One is washing or replacing the filter, depending on the type. The other is cleaning the evaporator and condenser coils.

To get at the mechanism, remove the front cover panel. Every make of air conditioner has a panel that is held with clips and can be lifted off, though some have catches or retainer screws that must be loosened first.

With the front cover off, clean the deflecting louvers with a dry cloth or brush. To reach the condenser coils and fins, pull the machine forward from the housing in which it rests on small wheels or runners.

If the conditioner is installed in the window so that most of the housing extends on the outside, and the metal case is securely fastened, it is all right to pull the machine forward as it will remain bal-anced. However, if the machine is only partly mounted into the wall and most of the case projects into the room take the precaution of placing a wooden box or other support under the case before drawing out the chassis, which is quite heavy.

Use a vacuum cleaner with the brush attachment to remove accumulated lint and dust, making sure the ventilator fins are clear for air passage.

If necessary, reverse the vacuum hose to blow dust out of the fins. Wipe the coils and meter housing with a clean damp cloth. Check the fan meter to see if it has any lubricating cups and if so, add oil. Even the "permanent" type of motor bearings should be given a few drops of #20 motor oil.

The filter is located directly behind the front louvers, extending all the way across so it can be lifted out from the top. The woven plastic or metal type is renewed by flushing under a faucet. Wash in detergent if the filter is greasy. The fiberglass type should be replaced with a new one at the start of each season, and again each month to insure maximum cooling benefits.

Check the wiring to see that the terminals are tight and the cord insulation undamaged. Then slide the mechanism back and replace the cover.

Now think back to last summer to recall any breakdowns or annoyances with that particular unit. Did the fuses blow every so often? Was there a tinny rattle or excessive vibration? Some of these conditions can be corrected or at least alleviated.

Best cure for an overloaded circuit is to bring in a separate line for the air conditioner. This is not necessarily an extensive job, as a separate circuit line can be carried directly to the room concealed inside the walls, or through a conduit attached outside along the house wall. But if your house has inadequate wiring, installation of a larger electrical service may be required, and is worthwhile for efficient use of modern appliances.

Noise problems may be inherent in the operation of the machine, but sometimes they result from a loose hinge or missing gasket on the exhaust door. The source can be tracked down by operating the machine with the cover off.

Vibration in the walls results when an installation is not adequately braced. If the matter is sufficiently bothersome, fit a brace under the machine and insulate with rubber or felt padding. In any event, the opening should be tightly caulked both inside and on the outside.

Conditioners installed in double-hung windows should be thoroughly checked to make sure that the supports are adequate and that the sash is tight so that it doesn't rattle when the machine is running.

A frequent cause of service calls is a worn electric receptacle which results in the uncertain contact with the plug prongs. Replace the receptacle with a new one, or get the locking type of plug that twists into the receptacle and can't be dislodged by vibration.   R.T.

▲ *Lift out filter located behind the condenser coils. Woven plastic type is cleaned under faucet. Other types should be replaced with new ones.*

◄ *Clean the air deflectors and casing with a brush or vacuum cleaner. Check the wire insulation and connections.*

▲ With machine cover off, clean compressor coils, housing, etc., thoroughly with vacuum hose and damp cloth.

▼ Check electric cord and wall receptacle, which are common causes of conditioner failure.

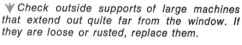

▲ Where necessary, reverse vacuum hose to blow out lint from evaporator fins, and inside the case. Wipe fan meter with cloth, apply a few drops of oil to bearings.

▼ Check outside supports of large machines that extend out quite far from the window. If they are loose or rusted, replace them.

> Following the classic design directive of "form follows function," this high-flying ultralight combines hang glider simplicity and conventional aircraft technology.

Discover the World of Ultralight Aircraft

These "poor man's flying machines" can become airborne from backyard landing strips

SEVENTY YEARS AGO, the daring young men and their flying machines captured the hearts and imaginations of many people too timid or wise to risk their own necks. Today, once again, flying in such flimsy contraptions is growing in popularity. But seven decades of aeronautical technology and the development of many new construction materials have made today's ultralight aircraft far safer than their pioneering prototypes.

Not that flying these modern flyweight machines is without risk. But that danger can be reduced to acceptable levels provided proper safety measures are observed.

Ultralights represent a step up from hang gliding, but ultralight aircraft are more than hang-gliding "kites" with makeshift motors attached. They are, in fact, true airplanes and the answer for those who cannot hang glide because of a lack of suitable launch sites. Instead of requiring a high cliff for launching, ultralights can take off from perfectly flat "backyard" airstrips half the length of a football field. Because the aircraft is engine-powered, the ultralight's pilot need not have the running legs needed for hang-gliding take-offs.

You need no pilot's license to fly *certain types* of ultralights because they are considered experimental planes. The dividing line between planes that do and do not require licensed operation is murky. The generally accepted rule is that if you can stand on your feet and personally support the plane during launchings, you need no license. But even if your ultralight is heavy enough to require wheeled support during

Discover the World of Ultralight Aircraft

take-offs and landings, you need only a student pilot's license and registration of the aircraft as a home-built machine.

You must also abide by Federal Air Regulation 91, Sub-part B, General Flight Rules. Moreover, your flying must be done only in fair weather, during daylight hours. Those are reasonable limitations because ultralights are basically constructed only for best-condition flying. You and everyone else will be a lot happier—and safer—if you stick to open pastures and small private airport landing strips as well. That is the situation today; what ultralight flying conditions and requirements will be a decade or two into the future is open to question.

Ultralight flyers have some remarkable accomplishments to their credit. Altitudes of some 18,000 feet and non-stop distances greater than 300 miles have already been achieved, and these records are bound to be broken. Such achievements are more impressive when the small size of these planes is appreciated. Forty-five different commercially available models have overall lengths ranging from a mere six feet (a Mitchell flying wing) to just under 27 feet. The average length is 19 feet. Empty weights range from 120 to 250 pounds, with an average weight of 170 pounds. Engine powers range from 10 to 30 HP, with an average around 18 HP. (The superlight GLA Minibat weighs in at only 80 pounds and uses a 3 HP engine. However, this plane is more a motorized glider than a true ultralight, although it is sometimes listed among ultralights along with other converted sailplanes and hang gliders.) See chart at end of article for other specification ranges.

▶ *Instrument panel for the ultralight aircraft on the opposite page. It contains air-speed indicator, tachometer and pull starter—all you need to fly. Pedals control the steerable tailwheel, and a snowmobile engine provides the push for a 38 mph cruise.*

The low weight of ultralight planes is attributable to the availability of light but tough construction materials, including polystyrene and fiberglass combinations, polyvinylchloride (PVC) plastic, Kevlar and carbon fiber fabrics. Many types of hardware (cables, pop-rivets and other fasteners) and glues (epoxies) hold the parts together reliably and with ease of application.

Aside from cost, the aspiring ultralight flier needs to know how long it takes on average to assemble a given kit, what special tools might be needed, how easily the completed plane can be folded or taken apart for transport to and from the flying area, and how much weather-protected home storage space is needed.

But the *stall speed* of any given plane is an even more important consideration. Stall speed indicates the point at which the plane experiences loss of lift and controllability because airflow that provides lift separates from the upper surface of the wing. To a point, the lower the stall speed the better off is the pilot. A low stall speed allows take-offs and landings on short runways. Moreover, a low stall speed makes

a possible crash landing less dangerous to both machine and pilot because the aircraft is moving ahead at relatively slow speed. However, top flying speed must usually be sacrificed to some degree to obtain a low stall speed. Stall speeds of 43 surveyed ultralight planes averaged 22.5 miles per hour.

When evaluating stall speeds of competing ultralight designs, the stall speed you will obtain might turn out to be a little higher than those indicated by the plane manufacturers, and that is because test flying conditions are usually different from your flying conditions. Also, you should determine whether the specified stall speeds relate to "free air" flights in which the planes are at least a wing-span distance above the ground. Closer than that, the plane actually achieves greater lift (hence a lower stall speed) because of an air-cushioning "ground effect."

Top flying speeds of the surveyed planes averaged 57 miles per hour, and the overall range extended from a mere 30 mph to 126 mph for the fastest. If you wish to estimate how long it would take to get from here to there in any given ultralight, you need to look at the substantially slower cruise speed which averages out to 43.7 mph for all surveyed planes.

Another thing you might like to calculate is whether you can get from here to there on one tankful of fuel. The maximum range is determined by fuel consumption, fuel capacity, and engine efficiency. The average range is 93.6 miles. A range of 360 miles was cited for one ultralight, and four models had only 20-mile trip potentials.

How far *up* can you go with these mini-planes? About half of the ultralight makers found no reason to boast about flight ceilings. The other half cited ceilings ranging from 3,000 to all of 18,000 feet, with the average working out to just under 11,000 feet.

How *fast* you can go up is also of considerable interest, especially if you suddenly see a grove of trees dead ahead. Climb rates for ultralights range from 75 to 900 feet per minute; the average climb rate is about 420 fpm.

How much runway space is needed to get a typical ultralight off and back onto the ground? The average take-off run is 170 feet, but for individual planes it can be as long as 750 feet or as short as 50 feet. Actual required space usually de-

▼ *This is a light, fast craft that can be assembled from a kit in one day.*

Foot-launched ultralight shown seconds after take-off. With this type of craft, pilot gains altitude before "retracting" his feet.

Adding tricycle landing gear to the craft makes take-off and landing easier and safer for the pilot. Aircraft performance is virtually unaffected. Wingtip rudders help make turns, along with elevons. With wheels, it can be conveniently walked to the flight line. Landing gear makes ground handling easier.

pends on the runway surface. For example, on hard surface a given plane might become airborne in 500 feet, yet require all of 900 feet when taking off from grass. Another factor is usable air space immediately after take-off. A plane might get off the ground in 50 feet, but if a 50-foot high obstacle must be avoided, the required runway might have to be more than six times longer! Space needed for a plane to complete its landing roll is often only a half or even a third as long as the runway space needed for take-off. The average landing roll is about 99 feet, while individual requirements range from 50 to as much as 300 feet.

Most ultralights have their power packs and propellers behind the wings and pilot so that they push rather than pull the aircraft. In a few instances, the props are out front as in more conventional flying machines.

Many types of small gasoline-fueled engines are used as power plants; most fall into the 10-to-20-horsepower range. Engines manufactured primarily for snowmobiles and go-carts are very popular. Some ultralight planes are fitted with twin engines that may be mounted separately at each side of the cockpit area to turn separate props; or they may be used to power two counter-rotating props on the same shaft. Counter-rotation helps prevent yaw (a deviation from the line of flight). An added degree of security is enjoyed if the plane is able to fly normally with only one of the two engines operational. It also would be possible to cruise with one engine to save on fuel. You may also run into an ultralight having a power plant intended only for take-off, in-flight restarts and climbing—and not for sustained flight.

Designers of ultralight planes spend much time and effort seeking new and more efficient wing designs. Wings currently in use range from the simplest of Rogollo-type sailwings used on hang gliders, to more elaborate structures that, for example, might have leading edges made of polyester/epoxy-covered polyfoam, ribs and bracing of Sitka spruce, and trailing edges of spruce or sheet aluminum. The ribs might also be of foam covered with bidirectional fiberglass held on with epoxy

cement. Sometimes a preshaped polyester bag is simply slipped over a framework of aluminum tubing and then pulled tight by use of simple tightening techniques. Another cost-cutting design involves applying a doped fabric (one finished with a varnishlike substance to waterproof and strengthen it) over a simple ladder-type framework. Wing coverings may be applied only to the top of the airfoil, or to both top and bottom for a fully "closed" wing structure. Wings usually are held in place with rigid struts of one kind or other, but sometimes they are wire-braced in the interest of weight reduction.

Most ultralights are of monoplane (one set of wings) design, but there are also some biplane (two sets of wings) designs that should appeal especially to those having nostalgic yearnings for the colorful first years of aviation. Even *tailless* biplanes have been designed and flown.

The body of an ultralight may be as complete as that of a fine sailplane, or be virtually nonexistent, consisting essentially of a framework of aluminum tubing able to support the pilot and engine pod. The fuselage might consist of a cockpit made of mahogany plywood, complete with padded seat, and a tailboom constructed of thin laminated wood or merely a large-diameter aluminum tube.

ULTRALIGHT AIRCRAFT STATISTICS			
These specification ranges reflect the characteristics of nearly 50 ultralight planes, including such borderline crafts as power-modified sailplanes and hang gliders.			
	Low	**High**	**Average**
Engine Horsepower	3 HP*	30 HP	18 HP
Length	6 ft.	27 ft.	19 ft.
Wing Span	17 ft.	42 ft.	33 ft.
Wing Area	65 sq. ft.*	188 sq. ft.	148 sq. ft.
Weight, Empty	80 lbs.*	250 lbs.	167 lbs.
Load	170 lbs.	400 lbs.	231 lbs.
Stall Speed	16 mph	40 mph	23 mph
Top Speed	30 mph	126 mph	57 mph
Cruise Speed	25 mph	75 mph	44 mph
Climb Rate (feet per minute at sea level)	75 fpm	900 fpm	420 fpm
Range	20 miles	360 miles	94 miles
Flight Ceiling	3,000 ft.**	18,000 ft.	11,000 ft.
Takeoff Run	50 ft.	750 ft.	170 ft.
Landing Roll	50 ft.	300 ft.	99 ft.

* Borderline ultralight (motorized glider)
** Many ultralights designed only for close-to-ground flying

A three-wheeled "tricycle" landing system is most generally used. It ordinarily consists of two large wheels plus a third smaller wheel that may be under the nose of the plane or near the tail section. Some nose wheels are movable for ease of taxiing, and may even have brakes. Tail wheels are sometimes replaced by simple skids.

When airborne, the pilot of a wheelless plane may sit on a simple seat, or be supported by some other type of harness. Seating in ultralights generally ranges from the simplest harnesses and open cockpits to completely enclosing, streamlined cockpits—especially on converted-to-power sailplanes.

In many ultralights, "steering" is accomplished by means of pilot body movements that change the crafts' centers of gravity. Body steering is generally used in ultralights that closely resemble or are in fact modified versions of hang gliders. The responses of ultralights to such controls range from docile to downright tricky.

Ultralights can be taken apart to varying degrees—and with varying speed and ease —for packing onto trailers, trucks or car tops. Some fold so compactly that they can be carried on the shoulders after detachment of the engine pods and be shoved into the cargo sections of station wagons.

A newcomer to ultralight flying would be well advised to investigate the advantages of joining the EAA Ultralight Association. EAA is the acronym for Experimental Aircraft Association. Benefits include participation in local chapter activities, organized fly-ins, a monthly publication, and insurance programs. For full information, write to: EAA Chapter Director, P.O. Box 299, Hales Corner, Wisconsin 53130.　　　　J.H.

What You Should Know about Burglar Alarms

Safeguarding your home successfully demands a knowledgeable approach— here's a review of the types of alarm systems available

Y OUR TELEPHONE RINGS, but goes unanswered because you are in the shower or away from home. Ten minutes later a stranger rings your doorbell. If you answer, he pretends to be looking for a friend in the neighborhood. If you do not answer the door, he will soon be inside, calmly taking his pick of your valuables.

Let's face facts. Lights left burning in an unoccupied house may discourage a wandering amateur housebreaker, but only the din of a burglar alarm upsets the pro.

The chance of your home being burglarized increases every year. Why be one of the victims when a good burglar alarm is known to be an effective deterrent to entry by someone who is after your worldly goods? It is the rare burglar, police say, who will risk remaining once an alarm has sounded and trying to turn it off; most prefer to get away quickly and look for an unprotected home.

Where formerly burglar-alarm protection was thought of as needed only in homes of heavily populated cities, the alarming rise in burglaries in the suburbs and even semi-rural areas has caused home owners there to have sophisticated electronic burglar alarm systems installed in their homes—many of which have paid for their desirable secluded locations by being burglarized, sometimes more than once.

A byproduct of this upsurge of breaking into homes is the growing number of businesses specializing in locks, alarms, steel doors, and installation of alarm systems.

Burglar alarms function with the activity of three elements. *Detectors* sense a presence and signal a *control center,* which sets off the *sounding* or *response device.*

What You Should Know about Burglar Alarms *71*

What type of alarm? Many different kinds of burglar alarm systems are available. Each type has advantages and disadvantages. So investigate all available systems carefully before deciding which is best for your particular needs. Remember that security problems vary with the different types of homes or apartment setups. So don't install an alarm system just because it works for a friend's home—it could be all wrong for yours. Study your home carefully in terms of security, and be guided accordingly.

Those simple little alarms that fasten directly to doors deserve only passing mention here since they offer minimal protection at best. They may be adequate for apartments, or in other homes where there are few avenues of entry.

More reliable systems include photoelectric devices, ultrasonic and microwave alarms, wired or wireless perimeter systems, and those that automatically telephone the police or anyone else of your choosing. A telephone system is the most expensive, but it may be the only wise choice for an isolated rural home where ordinary alarms would not be heard by neighbors or passersby.

An inexpensive photoelectric unit can protect only a limited area because triggering of the alarm depends on the breaking of a light beam by the intruder—meaning that it works only when an intruder has actually entered the home. Perhaps this is all the protection you need. However, bear these points in mind. First, give preference to a system that utilizes an invisible infrared beam and place the two units (light box and receiver) where the prowler cannot see them readily. If he spots the boxes, he can determine exactly where the light beam is whether it is invisible or not; he can then either crawl under or step over it. Secondly, consider only a unit having a *modulated* light source because only this type will work in lighted as well as dark

areas, and because it cannot be frustrated by the light from a burglar's flashlight. Finally, remember that the light beam must be where pet dogs and cats cannot intercept it.

One type of burglar alarm utilizes ultrasonic sound to trigger the detection signal. Such a unit consists of a single box placed in a strategic position from which it sends out a sound "pattern" that is inaudible to the human ear. The same unit also serves as a receiver. When an intruder steps into the sound area (about 100 square feet), he disturbs the pattern and sets off the alarm. These are good provided there is no air turbulence in the sound area. Cats and

▲ *A motion detector alarm is good for protecting specific areas of the home. It sounds an alarm in reaction to movement in the room. This one has been set on a wall between the ceiling and the top of the window for maximum effectiveness.*

▲ *The main control panel of an alarm system is usually set in a basement, stairwell, or closet. This places it out of the reach of an intruder who otherwise could turn it off.*

and another problem is that a vehicle or person passing by outside might set it off because microwaves can pass right through glass and dry walls.

Most motion detectors are equipped with controls that enable them to be "tuned" to the space they guard and adjusted to avoid false alarms, and most are self-contained boxes so that you can install one yourself. (Many can be moved to be used in different parts of the home at different times and can be taken along when you travel.) Be sure to place the alarm bell or siren where a burglar would have difficulty locating it and turning it off—especially away from the openings that are being protected.

dogs will activate the alarm, as will air currents created by heating or air-conditioning systems. Incidentally, dogs and cats *can* hear the sound even though you cannot, and they may not enjoy it.

If you have no wandering pets, and all you wish to do is protect one room and perhaps a staircase to the second floor, either the photoelectric or ultrasonic system may be a good choice. Both are quiet, efficient, and least troublesome to install and maintain.

Another of this type—they are in the category called *motion detectors*—is a microwave unit. More expensive than the ultrasonic or photoelectric unit, it works like radar and is a good choice for larger spaces, or where it might work better than an infrared or ultrasonic alarm because of air motion, temperature changes or noise. A microwave detector, however, can be activated by fluorescent lighting and vibrations,

▲ *Some burglar alarms are activated with this type of key pad as the family exits. Certain digits are punched in a specific sequence. This one has a red and a green light to indicate whether the alarm is on or off.*

What You Should Know about Burglar Alarms 73

➤ *In another type of alarm system, the switch in the door is depressed when the door is closed. Opening the door sets off the alarm. On a door regularly used for entrance and exit, the alarm can be set to lag ten seconds behind a door opening so that when the family members use it they have time before the alarm sounds to close the door or to shut off the alarm.*

A perimeter alarm system protects the outer edges of your living space, whether it is a house or an apartment. It does this by watching over points of entry—*accessible* windows and doors—and it requires a greater amount of installation than the motion detectors. All vulnerable openings are equipped with sensors that signal to a central control, which triggers an alarm device of your choice.

The sensors may be strung to the central control with low-voltage wires (an inexpensive if tedious process since the wiring of some systems can be rather elaborate), or the system may be wireless. Wireless detector-transmitters (one for each opening) and a wireless control are fairly expensive, but they save an enormous amount of bother stringing wires from door to door to window to control to response device.

The control box of a perimeter system is usually mounted near the front door—some outside, some inside. An indoor control should have a 30- to 40-second delay built in to allow time after turning on the system to leave and time after reentering to turn it off without causing the alarm to sound.

Outdoor-mounted controls are turned on with a switch in the box after you leave and turned off just before you reenter. A pair of wires can be run from the control through the house wall to an indoor control switch which you can use to arm the system when you are at home.

Most wired perimeter systems are relatively inexpensive—varying according to the home and type of installation. The wireless perimeter alarms are easier to install and much neater looking, but you pay for such convenience and appearance—up to four or five times as much as the wired types.

For a large house, with many windows and doors to be guarded, a combination perimeter-motion detector system can be utilized to avoid the excessive cost of equipping every opening with a sensor that must connect with or without wire to the central control.

The control center of your perimeter system should be provided with a backup battery supply—a power failure is precisely the time when you want to be sure your alarm system is working.

An advantage of the perimeter system is the variation it lends itself to in terms of the type of alert signal that may be used—depending on what works best for your family and situation. The response device can be a bell or a siren, or it can be lights

▲ *The strip of foil running around this window is yet another type of burglar alarm. If the window is broken, the foil is disturbed and triggers the alarm.*

About those stickers. Most burglars will leave a house alone if they are warned that an alarm system is in use. However, in some cases you should not use such warnings. If you live in a remote area and must rely on a warning system that automatically telephones the police, you should never advertise your security system. In this case you want the burglar to stick around until the police have time to respond to your call for help.

When your system is "go," tell your neighbors what the noise and signal light mean. You may wish to leave a duplicate cut-off key with a trusted neighbor so that the alarm can be turned off in your absence. Finally, let your police department know what kind of intruder protection you have.

We are all properly concerned about the rising incidence of "crime in the streets." Yet, statistically, the largest number of crimes are committed *off* the streets, as burglaries of homes and places of business. In this area, we can create some alarming situations for uninvited guests.

See also: ELECTRONICS.

that are rigged to go on or to flash. A telephone dialer can be programmed to dial someone—a neighbor, the police, a monitoring service—with a pre-recorded message that will sound the alert that your home has an intruder. (Check with your local police for possible restrictions on a dialing device.) These signal devices are more costly, of course, than a simple bell but if one of them suits your needs, it is well worth it.

Think like a burglar. After you have installed and tested your alarm system, go outside and study the house as a burglar might. Is there any way that you could frustrate the alarm system? Have you missed protecting any avenue of entry, such as a basement window? Can the warning light be seen from the street? Can the warning sound be heard by your neighbors? Did you place warning stickers where would-be intruders will see them?

WHERE TO FIND IT

For more information regarding components for simple perimeter alarm systems and motion detectors, consult catalogs of mail order radio-electronics supply houses such as Radio Shack, 2725 W. 7th St., Fort Worth, TX 76107, or visit their regional retail stores.

Professional quality burglar alarm supplies for do-it-yourselfers are available at Abco Supply, 387 Canal St., New York NY 10013, and A & H Burglar Alarms, 340 Canal St., New York, NY 10013.

Manufacturers of burglar alarm systems include BRK Electronics Div., Pittway Corp., 780 McClure Ave., Aurora, IL 60507; Master Lock Co., 2600 N. 32 St., Milwaukee, WI 53210; Mountain West, 4215 N. 16th St., Phoenix, AZ 85064; Notifier Co., 560 Alaska Ave., Torrance, CA 90503; Nutone Div., Scovill Mfg. Co., Madison & Redbank Rds., Cincinnati, OH 45227; Statitrol, Div. Emerson Electric Co., 140 S. Union Blvd., Lakewood, CO 80225; Universal Security Instruments, Inc., 10324 S. Dolfield Rd., Owings Mills, MD 21117.

Install a Burglar Alarm in Your Car

Shrill alarm sounds whenever trunk, hood or doors are tampered with

TWO HOURS of work and a modest invest- ment can put a theft alarm in your car that will sound whenever anyone tampers with the doors, trunk or hood. It will keep on sounding until you turn it off with a key.

In addition, the switch key on the fender next to the driver's door tells a would-be thief: "Careful. This car is wired for sound. Try something easier."

Unike some other alarms, this one can- not be silenced by a piece of tape holding down a trip switch or by the reclosing of an opened door. Turning it off requires either a key, or a hard yank on the right

wires. And, if the wires are concealed, no thief will want to take the time to find them while the siren is churning out its loud, shrill warning.

How it works. The schematic diagram shows how the siren and locking circuits work (also, see "Electronics"). M1, an electronic siren module, in conjunction with speaker SPKR, comprise the *siren*. The positive voltage input is fed through S1, a key-lock switch, to the module. R1 is sim- ply a dropping resistor for the module which works best with a 6- to 10-volt input.

The negative battery connection to the

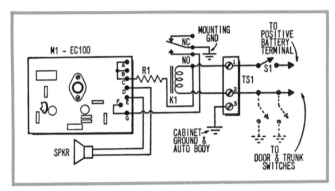

◄ *Noisemaker of the Auto Siren Sentry is the Eico EC 100 module (M1) that drives the speaker. Relay K1 keeps siren sounding even if car door is reclosed.*

siren module is made through normally closed pushbutton switches, like those used to turn on courtesy lights when a door is opened (these switches are indicated by the dotted lines in the schematic).

Trace the circuit through. Note that when a door is opened, the associated switch connects terminal 2 of terminal strip TS1 to ground—completing the power connection to the module and the siren "sounds off." Also note that when terminal 2 is grounded relay K1 is energized, pulling down K1's armature or wiper contact. When the moving contact touches this normally open terminal (#2) it parallels the door and trunk switches and "permanently" grounds the relay and the module's ground connection —the siren keeps sounding even if the door is closed (opening the switch). The only way K1 can be released—to turn off the *Auto Siren Sentry*—is by interrupting the positive battery connection by opening key switch S1.

Protecting the user. Since key-switch S1 is mounted on the fender—and you want it there for all to see—it protects the user against the embarrassment which might be caused by the siren going off as he attempts to leave the car (which will happen if the alarm switch is mounted inside the car). After the user leaves the car, the alarm is set by turning S1 to *on*. Before getting into the car, the driver then turns S1 to *off*. Naturally, if S1 is mounted inside the car the alarm will sound whenever the

driver enters the car. Mount the key switch out on the fender for your own peace of mind.

Construction. Actually there isn't much involved in building the *Auto Siren Sentry*. The siren module is an Eicocraft Siren Module Kit—type EC100, which can be assembled in a matter of minutes. There is but a handful of components which are mounted on a pre-punched and "component position marked" printed circuit board. However, assemble only the board itself, do not make the external connections given in the instructions; the *Auto Siren Sentry* uses a simpler external wiring than that given with the module.

After the module is completed, connect a 10-inch length of black wire to terminal *G*, loop the wire under the board and solder the end to *F*. Connect a one-inch length of bare wire to *C*. Connect a bare-wire jumper from point *A* to point *B*. Then connect two wires of the same color to *D* and *E*, the speaker terminals. Note that the board shows the battery conncetion to *A* and *B;* ignore these instructions. In the *Auto Siren Sentry* the positive battery connection is the short bare wire at *C* while the negative battery connection is the black wire going to *F* and *G*.

After all cabinet holes are cut in the main section of a 3 x 5 x 7-inch aluminum cabinet, mount the siren module as shown in the photographs, with the bottom as close as possible to one side; use stand-offs between the board and the cabinet to avoid shorting the printed-circuit wiring. The stand-offs as well as the necessary mounting hardware are supplied with the module.

The speaker is a three-inch waterproof type. The speaker specified in the Parts List is supplied in a metal cabinet having an integral gimbal bracket. If the speaker is installed as shown, in an aluminum cabinet, place a piece of perforated phenolic board in front of the speaker, to prevent possible damage to the cone. (If desired, the speaker can be used in the cabinet supplied.) Mount the speaker cabinet near the radiator, facing outwards, and connect the speaker leads from the module to the terminals on the speaker cabinet.

The wiper contact on K1 is *automatically grounded* when the relay is mounted in the cabinet—the wiper contact is connected directly to the frame of K1.

While only a three-lug terminal strip is required if the speaker is mounted in the aluminum cabinet, we show a five terminal type in the photographs to illustrate the arrangement when an external speaker is used. The speaker would connect to the two terminals shown unused. To reduce the possibility of wiring errors, place the battery connections on opposite ends of TS1, as shown, with at least the switch terminal in between.

Install the *Auto Siren Sentry* on any convenient surface under the hood. Just make certain the alarm doesn't project above hood line or you won't be able to close it.

Installing the switches. Any existing door switch automatically becomes part of the *Auto Siren Sentry* when the wire from terminal 2 of TS1 is connected to the courtesy light circuit. These switches are the self-grounding type, always switching the ground lead of the courtesy lights: therefore, when you look at these switches you will see only *one* connecting wire. All other

switches which may be added should be of the same type, self-grounding, with their leads connected to the wiring of any of the original door switches. Additional switches for the hood, trunk or rear doors can be purchased from your car dealer at nominal cost.

The key switch should be installed so some smart "cooky" can't jump the terminals. If the switch is installed in the part of the fender that faces the tire anyone can reach under the car and jump the terminals, making the alarm inoperative. Install the switch on part of the *double fender*. Part of each fender, near the door, is shielded by the sides of the firewall, and access to the space between the fender and firewall is only through a small area which is exposed when the door is open. Place the switch so that its terminals are in the concealed space.

Positive grounds. The circuit shown is for cars with the more common *negative* ground battery. If your car uses a positive ground battery simply reverse the connections to siren module terminals C and G.

Six-volt systems. If your car uses six-volts, eliminate R1—use a direct connection from terminal 1 of TS1 and use the alternate six-volt relay specified in the parts list.   H.F.

See also: ELECTRONICS.

PARTS LIST — Construction Time: 2 hours	
K1	S.p.d.t. relay (Potter and Brumfield RS5D—12VDC, Allied 41D5504—P&B RS5D-6VDC—Allied 41D5896 or equivalent)
M1	Siren Module EC 100 or equivalent
R1	10-ohm, 5 watt resistor
Spkr	Weatherproof speaker (Lafayette 44C-5201 or equivalent)
TS1	Terminal Strip
	3 x 5 x 7 inch aluminum chassis box
Misc.	Wire, solder, mounting hardware, solder jugs, etc.

Burglar-proof Your Car's Tape Player

This alarm requires only four components, and you can install it quickly

MOST of the fancy tape player lock-alarms are useless—they are too obvious, too easily bypassed, and are often stolen along with the tape player. Our Auto-Alarm sounds a car's horn continuously if anyone removes the tape player. And once triggered, the horn can be turned off only by the AutoAlarm's switch.

All it takes is a few dollars worth of experimenter's components to throw together an AutoAlarm that will give you just about as much protection as you can get because it doesn't *look* like an alarm. Tucked away in the glove compartment or under the seat, a single wire runs to the tape player's case—a wire that looks as if it's an ordinary ground wire.

The entire AutoAlarm is assembled directly on the back of a SPST slide switch. The assembly can then be installed in any small metal or plastic cabinet. Silicon Controlled Rectifier SCR1 can be just about

any type rated at 25 PIV (peak inverse volts), 5-Amps or higher, such as the HEP-R1220.

To identify the SCR leads, lay it flat on

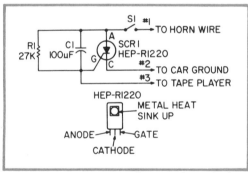

▲ *This simple circuit can be wired quickly. Switch S1 is closed for normal operation.*

PARTS LIST	
C1	100-uF electrolytic capacitor 15 VDC or better
R1	27,000-ohms, ½-watt resistor
SCR1	HEP-R1220 or equivalent
S1	SPST slide switch (alarm off)
Misc.	Metal or plastic cabinet, wire, hardware, solder, etc.

Burglar-proof Your Car's Tape Player   *79*

the table so the side with the metal rim (around the mounting hole) faces up; the side *without* a rim should be against the table. The SCR leads will now conform to the layout shown.

No wiring precautions are necessary other than to doublecheck that the C1 polarity is correct; its positive terminal connects to SCR1's anode (A) terminal.

The other figure shows how to connect the AutoAlarm. Note that AutoAlarm wire #2, from SCR1's cathode, must connect to the car body (ground) while the #3 wire also connects to ground *but* through the tape player's case. Wire #1 connects to the horn control wire which generally enters at the bottom of the steering column (sometimes in the engine compartment, sometimes under the dash).

How it works. There is a positive voltage from the car battery across a horn button when it is open. By closing the horn button, the circuit is completed and the horn will sound. This positive voltage is applied to SCR1's anode. The SCR's gate is grounded through the tape player's case, so the SCR is normally off. When the tape player is removed from its mount, the AutoAlarm's #3 wire is disconnected from ground. The SCR gate is no longer grounded, so current can flow through R1 to the gate. The SCR turns on, effectively short-

ing its anode to its cathode. This means the horn control wire is now grounded, so the horn will sound.

Once the horn is sounded it can only be turned off by opening switch SW1.

To make it easy for the thief to trigger the AutoAlarm we suggest that the #3 wire be 22 or 24 gauge stranded—thin enough to be easily broken when the player is removed. The #1 and #2 wires should be 18 gauge stranded.   H.F.

See also: ELECTRONICS.

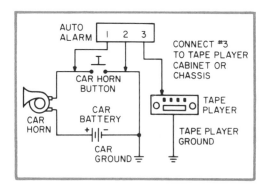

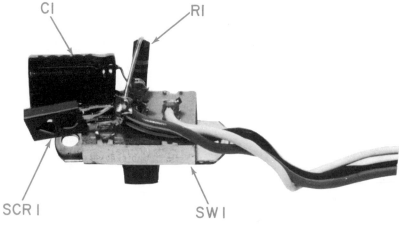

▲ *Intermediate solenoid found on most autos in place of horn in our simple diagram does not alter operation. Connect #1 to button. Remember, the curved side of electrolytic capacitor symbols, such as C1, represents the terminal that must be connected to the negative voltage (with respect to the plus capacitor connection). In this circuit, it means the negative terminal of capacitor C1 must be connected to the gate terminal of Silicon Control Rectifier SCR1 at left.*

CI   RI

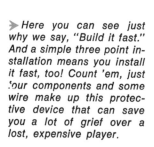

➤*Here you can see just why we say, "Build it fast." And a simple three point installation means you install it fast, too! Count 'em, just four components and some wire make up this protective device that can save you a lot of grief over a lost, expensive player.*

SCR I   SW I

Let Cyclops
Keep an Eye on
Your Home

This electronic burglar alarm is activated by light—you can buy it or build it yourself, and here's how

THE NEED FOR A BURGLAR ALARM in the home hardly needs to be championed these days, and one of the newer and better ones now available is Cyclops, a light-sensitive device that sounds a musical alarm if an intrusion should occur. Happily for energy-conscious users, it does so on a meager electrical supply—using only one-half watt when working. If the Cyclops alarm is activated by an intruder, once it has sounded the device resets itself to continue the job of home surveillance.

The eye and heart of Cyclops is a specialized integrated circuit (IC) which is the result of a marriage between a photodiode and a digital and linear circuit on a single chip. Such a device is called an Optolinear and is available to you from the source specified at the end of this article. This is the 14-pin IC chip shown in the photograph of the completed Cyclops printed circuit (PC) board on page 84 and is referred to hereafter as IC1.

IC1 is an integrated circuit motion detector which monitors the ambient light in-

tensity falling on the built-in photodiode. When a change in light intensity occurs, a circuit is triggered which produces a series of pulses of varying frequency in the audio range. Current in the loudspeaker is zero. When IC1 is activated, Q2 conducts current and provides base drive to Q5 through R3, for which the circuit is set for maximum volume. Q5 acts as a switching transistor, driving the loudspeaker with pulses of about 12 volts. The circuit will drive loudspeakers of any impedance. Greatest volume will be obtained with a 3.2 ohm speaker, since this will draw the highest load current from Q5. Peak power delivered to a 3.2 ohm speaker can be as high as 40 watts when the volume control is set to maximum. Average power will be much less than this since the circuit delivers pulses with a duty cycle of less than 50 percent.

Construction procedures. Cyclops can be constructed on a single sided printed circuit board measuring 2⅞ by 4¼ inches. This includes all the necessary circuitry except the 12-volt power source. If an AC-operated power supply is desired, it can be added to the circuit at the option of the builder. A typical power supply circuit is shown with the diagram.

The printed circuit pattern in this article is shown as seen from the copper side of the printed circuit board. The parts location diagram is also shown. If possible,

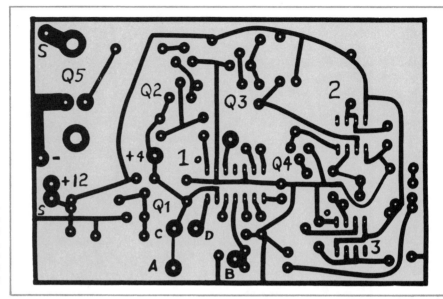

▶ *Full-sized printed circuit board template to use in making your own Cyclops burglar alarm. Printed circuit kits are available with materials for lifting patterns from a printed page.*

make photocopies of the printed circuit, parts diagram, and schematic diagram and work from these copies. This will avoid wear and tear on the originals which you will want to keep in good condition for future reference.

After etching the printed circuit, go over it with a magnifying glass to pick up any shorts or opens which may exist. This will help avoid problems when the circuit is first placed in operation. For a slight additional cost, it is strongly recommended that sockets be used for placement of the integrated circuits. Their value in a printed circuit assembly cannot be overemphasized. The use of sockets gives you the ability to troubleshoot the circuit, should a problem exist, in much less time than if the integrated circuits were soldered in place. It is extremely difficult to remove a multipin IC which has been soldered into a printed circuit without destroying the IC or printed circuit. Do not mount the integrated circuits until instructed to do so in the checkout procedure.

The parts diagram shows control switch S1 and volume control R3 mounted di-

rectly to the printed circuit board. You may want to mount the printed circuit board in a small cabinet with these components accessible from the outside. If you are going to use the lamp with the circuit, be sure to place it so that its light will not fall upon IC1. Should this happen, the additional feedback signal from the lamp may cause a circuit malfunction, although no damage will occur.

You will note that the power output transistor, Q5, is mounted to the printed circuit board with no heat sink. None is required since this transistor operates as a switch at high current levels, and therefore dissipates very little heat. Mount Q5 to the printed circuit board with two 4-40 screws and nuts. Make them tight but not overtight.

Checkout procedures. The printed circuit assembly should be checked with power applied before installing any of the integrated circuits in place. This will avoid damaged components in the event of possible short circuits or miswiring. Apply 12 VDC power to the circuit using a battery or AC-operated power supply, observing

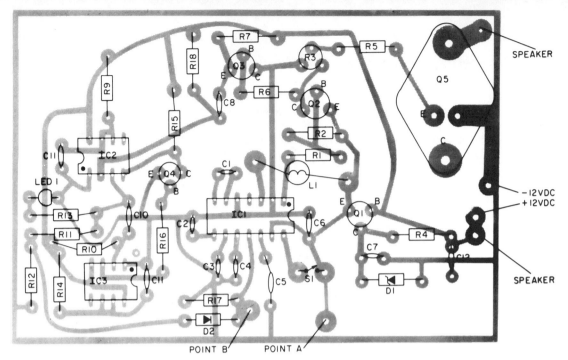

▲ Parts location diagram for printed circuit. View is from component side, parts facing up. Foil PC patterns are on the underside.

correct polarity. Measure the voltage at pin 13 of IC1 using the negative side of the DC power supply as the meter reference. This should be between +3.5 and +4.5 volts DC. If the voltage is not within this range, check zener diode D1 for a voltage drop of 4.2 to 5.2 volts. Check also that D1 is mounted so that the cathode side is connected to the base of Q1. Do not proceed further until the voltage at pin 13 of IC1 is within the range of +3.5 to 4.5 volts.

Measure the voltage at pins 2, 5, 6, 7, 8, 9, 10, and 12 of IC1. This voltage should be zero. Measure the voltage at pin 8 of IC2 and IC3. This voltage should be about +12 volts. Measure the voltage at pin 1 of IC2 and IC3. This voltage should be zero.

Disconnect the power from the circuit. Very carefully insert the integrated circuits in their sockets, paying strict attention to the proper orientation for pin 1 as shown in the parts layout. Pin 1 of the Opto-linear IC is indicated by a red dot or "U"-shaped indentation molded into the top of the plastic case at one end.

Be sure the speaker is properly connected to the circuit between the +12 volt bus and the collector of Q5. Set A digital counter within the chip permits a specified number of pulses to be generated, and then resets the circuit back to a standby mode to await the next change in light intensity falling upon the photodiode. The series of audio pulses produced, when amplified and fed to a loudspeaker, is a simulation of the familiar whooping sound which is characteristic of some alarms. C4 determines the rate at which the circuit changes from one tone to the next, and can be changed to suit individual tastes. IC1 has an additional digital circuit which produces a second set of random musical tones which might be described as "Close Encounters" music. When the chip is in this mode of operation, it is also capable of flashing a 6 volt light bulb in time with the music.

Control of the operation of IC1 is accomplished by feeding a positive voltage to either or both control input terminals, pins 11 and 14. When terminals C and D of the printed circuit are connected together and terminals A and B are open, the cir-

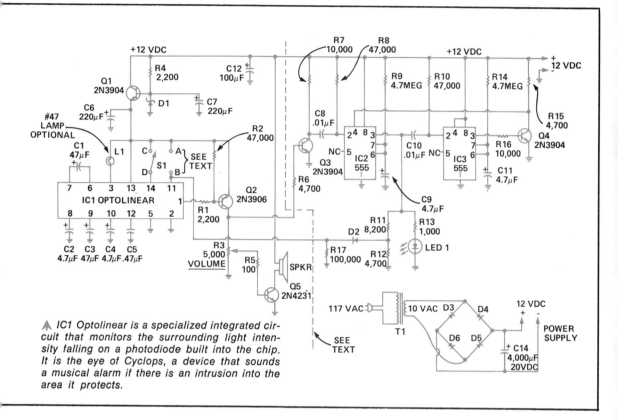

▲ IC1 Optolinear is a specialized integrated circuit that monitors the surrounding light intensity falling on a photodiode built into the chip. It is the eye of Cyclops, a device that sounds a musical alarm if there is an intrusion into the area it protects.

PARTS LIST		
C1, C3	47 µF electrolytic capacitor, 10 VDC	
C2, C4	4.7 µF electrolytic capacitor, 10 VDC	
C5	0.47 µF ceramic disc capacitor, 10 VDC	
C6, C7	220 µF electrolytic capacitor, 20 VDC	
C8, C10	0.01 µF ceramic capacitor, 10 VDC	
C9, C11	4.7 µF electrolytic capacitor, 20 VDC	
C12	100 µF electrolytic capacitor, 20 VDC	
C14	4,000 µF electrolytic capacitor, 20 VDC	
D1	1N5230 4.7 volt zener diode	
D2	1N4148 silicon diode	
D3, D4, D5, D6	1N2069 silicon diode	
IC1	Optolinear IC (see text)	
IC2	555 timer	
IC3	555 timer	
L1	#47 lamp	
LED1	light emitting diode	
Q1, Q3 Q4	2N3904 NPN silicon transistor	
Q2	2N3906 PNP silicon transistor	
Q5	2N4231 NPN silicon transistor	
R1, R4	2,200-ohm, 1/4-watt resistor	
R2, R8, R10	47,000-ohm, 1/4-watt resistor	
R3	5,000-ohm trimmer potentiometer (PC board mounting type)	
R5	100-ohm, 1/4-watt resistor	
R6, R12, R15	4,700-ohm, 1/4-watt resistor	
R7, R16	10,000-ohm, 1/4-watt resistor	
R9, R14	4,700,000-ohm, 1/4-watt resistor	
R11	8,200-ohm, 1/4-watt resistor	
R13	1,000-ohm, 1/4-watt resistor	
R17	100,000-ohm, 1/4-watt resistor	
SPKR	3.2-ohm PM type speaker	
S1	SPST miniature slide switch	
T1	10-volt, 1.2 amp transformer	
Misc.	8x4x4" plastic cabinet, screws, spacers, wire, AC plug and zip cord, etc.	

◄ Completed printed circuit board. Optolinear IC chip, the eye of the Cyclops, is in the upper center. It detects small changes in ambient light and triggers alarm.

cuit is set to perform as an intrusion alarm. Opening the circuit between terminals C and D, and A and B, programs the circuit for "Close Encounters" music. Automatic control of terminals A and B of the circuit is provided by IC2 and IC3, and manual control of terminals C and D is provided by a single pole slide switch mounted directly on the printed circuit board.

Power to drive a loudspeaker is provided by Q2 and Q5 which amplify the low voltage output pulses of IC1 and deliver peak currents of up to 1 ampere into the speaker. When IC1 is in standby mode, the voltage at the output terminals, pin 1, is about 4 volts. This cuts off both Q2 and Q5 so that S1 is thrown to the ON or closed position. Adjust the volume control about halfway and apply 12 volts of power to the circuit, observing correct polarity. You should hear the whooping sound generated by the circuit, and the light-emitting diode (LED) should light. The LED should remain lit for about 30 seconds, and when it goes out, the sound should continue for a few seconds more. Once the sound stops, you can wave your hand over IC1 and cause the sound to start again. This time the circuit will reset itself after a few seconds, since IC2 is being inhibited by the timed cycle of IC3. After another 30 seconds has passed, the cycle can be repeated.

To generate the "Close Encounters" music sound, throw S1 to the OFF or open position. When you apply power to the circuit, Cyclops will generate the whooping sound for 30 seconds, and then will switch to the "Close Encounters" music for another 30 seconds as IC2 and IC3 switch on and off. This sequence will repeat indefinitely. If you wish to generate only the "Close Encounters" sound, remove IC2.

Cyclops can be used in many applications depending upon the connections between terminals A, B, C, and D of the circuit and whether or not the timing circuitry of IC2 and IC3 is included in the assembly.

A combination whooping sound and "Close Encounters" music can be produced by building the entire circuit and setting S1 to the OFF or open position. Delete the timing circuit for continuous "Close Encounters" music.

See also: ELECTRONICS; HOME SECURITY SENSORS.

WHERE TO FIND IT

The specialized Optolinear integrated circuit for the Cyclops burglar alarm (IC1 in diagram) may be purchased from Delta Electronics, 7 Oakland Street, P.O. Box 2, Amesbury, MA 01913. Ask for #1072W in their catalog.

For those who do not have the time or experience to build a Cyclops, an assembled unit may also be purchased from Delta Electronics.

➤This is the utimate in charging systems—an alternator with built-in voltage regulation.

Maintaining Alternator Output

This job is advanced for a novice, but an experienced weekend mechanic can handle it

VIRTUALLY ALL CARS built in recent years (Volkswagen a notable exception) have AC generators, commonly called alternators.

The alternator electrical system represents a high achievement in obtaining the most electrical power from a minimum draw on engine output. It has been termed the ultimate electrical power source for automotive use.

The alternator offers the potential for longer battery life in addition to its primary advantage—higher output. The higher output is due to the comparatively low weight of the rotor and coil assembly allowing greater pulley ratios for higher rpm. The result, of course, is higher output—even at engine idle. Maintaining the advantage an alternate gives your electrical system is just a matter of knowing the alternator and keeping it in top tune.

Construction. All alternators consist of a stator, which corresponds to the generator's field circuit, and a rotor, which corresponds to the generator's armature. The only essential difference between the two is the method used to convert alternating current to direct current. Alternator construction can be seen in the accompanying illustrations.

In generators, as you've seen, brushes are used to pick the alternating current off a commutator, converting that current to direct. Alternators, however, employ silicon rectifiers or, for short, diodes. Don't be confused by the fact that alternators also contain brushes because they are used for a different purpose than in a generator. Alternator brushes supply field current to the rotor by connecting two slip rings mounted concentrically on the rotor shaft.

The rectifier in the alternator is a chemical disc that changes alternating current to direct current since it permits current to

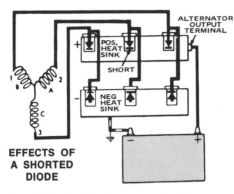

EFFECTS OF A SHORTED DIODE

Shorted diode will allow current to flow in both directions. It will flow back to the A winding instead of to the battery.

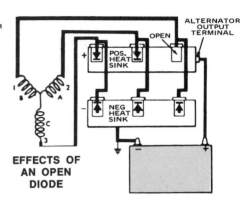

EFFECTS OF AN OPEN DIODE

Open diode will not let current flow in either direction. The circuit is not complete through the B winding to battery.

▲ *The diode, also called rectifier, converts the AC output of the alternator into DC by permitting current to flow only one way.*

flow in one direction only. In other words, the rectifiers used in alternators have a low resistance to the flow of electrical current in one direction and a high resistance to the flow of electrical current in the other direction.

This low resistance allows current to flow from the alternator to the battery, but the rectifier's high resistance prevents a return flow from the battery to the alternator when battery current exceeds alternator output, as it does when the engine idles.

Both alternator and generator have regulator units, but the makeup of each is different. One difference is the absence of a circuit breaker (the cut-out relay) in the alternator regulator.

In the generator's regulator, as you've seen, the circuit breaker connects and disconnects the battery and generator at the proper time. Since the alternator is self-rectifying, though, allowing current to flow only in one direction—toward the battery—there is no need for a circuit breaker. The constant, steady flow of current from the alternator to the battery allows the battery to maintain a full state of charge.

Another difference is the absence of a current regulator. The alternator cannot overcharge so long as the voltage regula-

tion is correct, so there is no need for other than a voltage regulator.

The simple requirements of the alternator for regulation hastened the development of the fully-electronic voltage regulator.

Now used on virtually all cars with alternators, the fully-electronic regulator has no vibrating contacts and is not adjustable. Either it works or it doesn't, and it usually does.

On most cars, the fully electronic regulator is either a plug-in to the alternator or built into it.

The service information in this article on voltage regulators, therefore, refers to the vibrating contact type used mostly in older car models.

Maintenance. The alternator is no harder to tune than the generator. If trouble is apparent, you don't usually have to replace the entire unit. The unit breaks into two parts—the stator and rotor—allowing you to replace the one that is giving the trouble.

In many cases, you don't even have to replace one of those major components. A common problem, low output, is normally traced to either of two things: a slipping fan belt or defective diodes (rectifiers).

Fan belt tension is critical with the

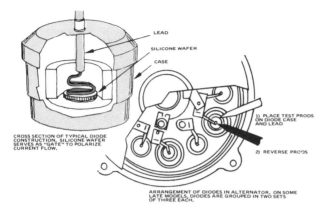

LEAD

SILICONE WAFER

CASE

CROSS SECTION OF TYPICAL DIODE CONSTRUCTION, SILICONE WAFER SERVES AS "GATE" TO POLARIZE CURRENT FLOW.

1) PLACE TEST PRODS ON DIODE CASE AND LEAD

2) REVERSE PRODS

ARRANGEMENT OF DIODES IN ALTERNATOR, ON SOME LATE MODELS, DIODES ARE GROUPED IN TWO SETS OF THREE EACH.

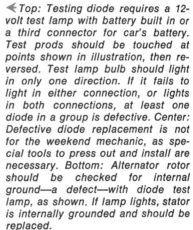

◄ Top: Testing diode requires a 12-volt test lamp with battery built in or a third connector for car's battery. Test prods should be touched at points shown in illustration, then reversed. Test lamp bulb should light in only one direction. If it fails to light in either connection, or lights in both connections, at least one diode in a group is defective. Center: Defective diode replacement is not for the weekend mechanic, as special tools to press out and install are necessary. Bottom: Alternator rotor should be checked for internal ground—a defect—with diode test lamp, as shown. If lamp lights, stator is internally grounded and should be replaced.

▼ Alternator output test requires an ammeter and voltmeter, connected as shown, and a fully-charged battery. Carbon pile is a load-adjusting rheostat, but you can also load battery by turning on accessories and lights. For this test, disconnect battery cables and alternator connections. On some GM Delcotron alternators, field terminal has "2" below it; on all others, the letter "F" is used. When fully loaded, alternator should put out within three amps of specifications. If five amps or more below specifications, bad diode is indicated.

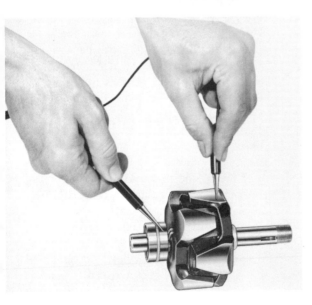

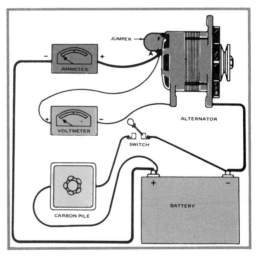

JUMPER

AMMETER

VOLTMETER

SWITCH

ALTERNATOR

CARBON PILE

BATTERY

alternator. Always make sure the belt is in good condition and adjusted to specification.

The one precaution you must keep in mind when working with the alternator is guarding against reverse polarity. Reverse the polarity of the alternator or the battery for even an instant and you stand a chance of burning out the rectifiers. To prevent accidental grounding, furthermore, you should always use insulated tools when working in the area of the alternator.

Following adjustment of the fan belt, turn your attention to the regulator. Make sure all connections at this unit are tight. Follow this by checking the condition of the regulator points. If you find they're burned or pitted, you'll have to replace the regulator. Now, check and tighten all connections including those to the ignition switch, the ballast resistor, the regulator and the conducting surfaces of the fuse and holder.

Unscrew the brushes from the alternator and inspect them for wear. If worn, replace them.

In some cars, the brushes can be removed from the alternator with the unit in the car. This is done by unscrewing the external cap screws to which the brushes are attached. In other cars, the unit must be removed from the car to reach the brushes, which can then be unscrewed.

If it becomes necessary to take the unit apart, remove it from the car and split it open, separating the stator from the rotor. Test the rectifiers first. This can be done with a commercial diode tester, although you can also use any continuity tester, such as an ohmmeter or a test lamp that plugs into household current. The test connections are illustrated.

If a diode is defective, it must be replaced. This requires special tools and should be left to a professional shop.

Next inspect the stator wiring carefully for breaks. To be absolutely sure there are none, you should test from the stator leads to the stator core with a 110-volt test lamp or other suitable tester. If the lamp lights, the stator is grounded and should be replaced.

Finally, test the field windings in the rotor part of the alternator. This is done with an ammeter hooked to the alternator battery output terminal while turning the rotor shaft by hand. The correct field current draw should be recorded on the meter. This reading differs from car to car, so check your service manual.

The above description tells you what to do if you are not getting output from the alternator. However, there are things a faultily adjusted or malfunctioning alternator can cause—most can be checked on the car.

Low charging rate. A low charging rate is indicated when the ammeter or trouble light in your car begins to show discharge at low engine speed and idle. It is also indicated if a battery gets run-down.

Look at the fan belt first and make sure it's properly adjusted. Then check the battery terminals where high resistance could be causing the trouble. Remove the cables and clean the terminals and posts. Make sure the ground cable is clean and tight.

Finally, check at the alternator for loose connections. If the trouble still persists, replace the brushes in the alternator since poor contact between brushes and slip rings is a major factor for a low charging rate. As a final tuneup procedure, remove the alternator from the car and check the stator. Open windings cause an unsteady low charging rate.

If the ammeter trouble light flicks on and off at all speeds and you get a run-down battery, which indicates low voltage output, check the regulator first. To do this, hook the negative lead of a voltmeter to the battery's negative post and the positive to the positive post. Connect a jumper wire from the ignition terminal to the field terminal on the regulator and then start the engine. The voltmeter should read about 14 to 15 volts for a 12-volt charging system. If not, the regulator is faulty. Try adjusting the regulator points; if that does not increase the voltage output, get a new regulator.

But if the regulator does check out, go to the alternator and tighten all connections. The trouble could also be a shorted rectifier or grounded stator, so check them as well.

High charging rate. It is possible for the alternator to throw out too much charge. An over-charge condition will show up by acid salts on the battery and the battery beginning to use too much water. Check the regulator first; if it's set too high, adjust the points. If this doesn't help, don't scrap the regulator yet.

First remove the unit and clean its mounting surface. A poorly grounded regulator could be causing the problem. If not, the problem is either that the regulator points are stuck or that there are open windings in the unit. If so, replace the regulator.

If the battery is using too much water or a lot of acid salts begin to form, it could also mean that the regulator points are oxidizing. The cause could be a loose or dirty ground connection, so clean the mounting surface and tighten all attaching bolts. Now, test the regulator. If the meter shows a high voltage, set the points.

Finally, check and adjust the regulator air gap to specification as given in your car's manual. To do this, connect a test lamp between the regulator ignition and field terminals. Insert the proper wire gauge (one of .048 inch). Press the armature plate down. The contacts should open and the test lamp should dim.

Now, insert a larger wire gauge in the same position (usually one of .052 inch). Depress the armature plate. The upper contact should be closed and the test lamp should remain lighted. If the air gap doesn't check out, adjust it by bending the upper contact support until you get the right openings and test readings.

Another reason for oxidized points could be shorted field windings in the rotor pole. In this case, the rotor has to be replaced.

Again, excessive use of water by the battery and acid salts on the battery are indications of another condition—burned regulator points. The trouble is probably a regulator set too high or shorted field windings in the rotor pole. In the former case, adjust the points—in the latter, replace the rotor.

Mechanical problems. An alternator that is noisy is one that is either loose on its mountings or one that has internal problems. First check the mounting bolts and make sure the alternator is tightly connected. The drive pulley could also be causing the noise, so ensure that it is tight.

If this fails to stop the noise, remove the alternator from the car and break it open. Inspect the rotor fan blades. If bent, replace the rotor. Now test each rectifier for a short. If this doesn't stop the trouble, the problem is a sprung rotor shaft, worn shaft bearings or open or shorted windings in the stator and a rubbing rotor pole.

In the event of a sprung rotor shaft, replace the rotor. If the problem boils down to worn shaft bearings, you can have them replaced too. If, though, the stator windings are shorted and the rotor poles are rubbing, you'll have to replace the entire alternator.

If the battery keeps running down for no rhyme or reason, it indicates that the regulator points are stuck closed. This was probably caused by a poor ground connection between the alternator and regulator. Replace the regulator and make sure the new unit is properly grounded so the trouble doesn't recur. P.W.

See also: ENGINE; ELECTRICAL, AUTO.

How to Make Screens and Storm Windows

Do the job yourself with inexpensive aluminum components and a few simple tools

▲ *Completed screen is hung from brackets at top and held by hook and eye fasteners at the bottom.*

ONE EASY and satisfying way to save money on home maintenance and improvement is to make your own interchangeable window screens and storm sashes using maintenance-free aluminum construction materials that are available at any large hardware store. Only a few simple hand tools are needed.

The following discussion applies primarily to the making of full-size screens for installation on conventional double-hung windows. But screens for any other type of window can be made as easily, following the additional tips provided at the end of this article. Surprisingly, constructing storm sashes is even more of a breeze than making the screens. The only important point to bear in mind is that you need one type of framing material to hold screening, and a different type for glass (see diagram). The corner locking pieces and hanger units are identical in each case.

To avoid wasting material, rough-measure your window height and width to determine whether the six- or eight-foot lengths of framing material will be more economical. Re-measure the windows just outside the blind stops more carefully when you are ready to cut the framing to

proper size. Make the vertical and horizontal sections all ⅛-inch shorter than the actual window measurements to avoid an over-tight fit. After removing the U-shaped spline that locks in the screening, mark 45-degree angles at the measured points so that the edge forming the channel accepting the spline becomes the shorter of the two sides. Cut accurately along the 45-degree lines using a hacksaw. If you plan to make many screens and/or storm sashes, the construction of a simple miter box (see photo) will save much time and ensure precise cuts. De-burr the cut ends with a file or sandpaper.

To assemble the frame, push a corner lock into each end of one short side, add vertical members to the exposed portions of the corner locks, and finish off by pushing on the other end piece to which corner locks have been added. Check all corners to make sure they form good right angles. The frame is now ready for addition of the screening if the screen area is six square feet or less. A cross brace should be added to larger screens, as shown. Just notch back two ends of a length of framing material to form ⅝-inch lips to overlap the basic frame. Drill a hole

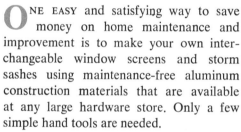

in each lip to accept a #6 ⅜-inch aluminum sheet metal screw, and smaller pilot holes in appropriate positions on the frame. Note that the screening is *not* attached to this brace.

During the following operations, make certain that the weave of the screening runs parallel to the frame channels, and try to cut carefully between two adjacent screen wires to help keep the screening square. Ordinary household shears can be used to cut the screening.

Start by aligning the selvedge edge, or a pre-cut straight edge, along one long channel so that the screening just covers the channel opening. When this edge is pressed into the channel later, it will fit down against the inside edge of the groove *only*; do not allow it to run across the bottom of the channel. While holding the screen in place, cut about two inches up an adjacent side, then snip a small triangular bit of screening off the corner to avoid bunching inside the channel.

Use an ordinary putty knife to press the selvedge or pre-cut edge into the groove. This is easier if you lay a strip of ¼-inch thick plywood above and below the screen as shown. Try to obtain a neat right-angle bend. Lock this edge of screen-

MATERIALS FOR SCREENS	
	Reynolds No.
Aluminum screen framing complete with spline:	
6 ft. lengths	6046
8 ft. lengths	6047
Corner locks (4 per frame)	7210
Hangers (2 units per frame)	7214
Aluminum screen cloth	
Small hooks with screw-eyes (2 each per frame)	

ing in place by inserting the proper length of spline which has been square-cut to run the full length of the channel. Tighten the spline by tapping a length of ¼-inch thick plywood laid atop the spline. To avoid dents, slightly round the edges and ends of the plywood.

Before cutting and locking in the other edges in the same manner, place some scraps of aluminum framing, or wood scraps of the same thickness, under the screening to keep it from sagging during the finishing operations. Cut the screening along the two short edges so that the edges can be shaped neatly along the inside walls of the channels. Lock in place with splines, and then complete assembly of the fourth side in the same manner.

◄*Aluminum screens and storm windows are assembled in about the same way, but screen uses a different frame member (left) than the storm window (right).*

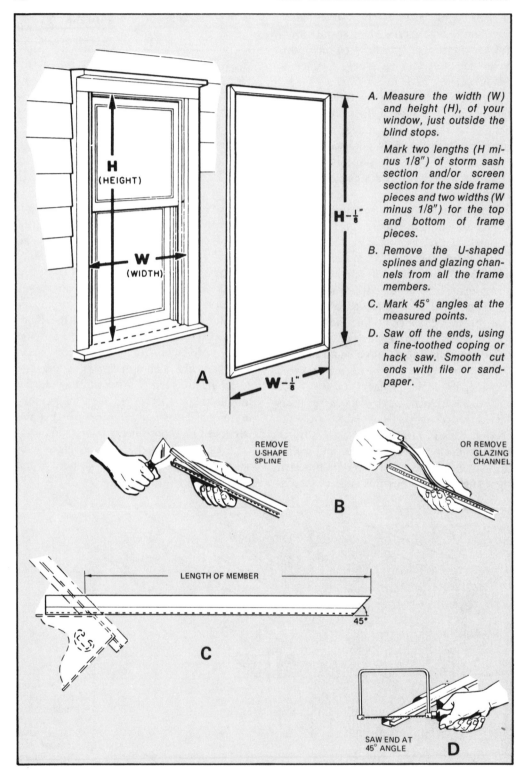

A. Measure the width (W) and height (H), of your window, just outside the blind stops.

Mark two lengths (H minus 1/8") of storm sash section and/or screen section for the side frame pieces and two widths (W minus 1/8") for the top and bottom of frame pieces.

B. Remove the U-shaped splines and glazing channels from all the frame members.

C. Mark 45° angles at the measured points.

D. Saw off the ends, using a fine-toothed coping or hack saw. Smooth cut ends with file or sandpaper.

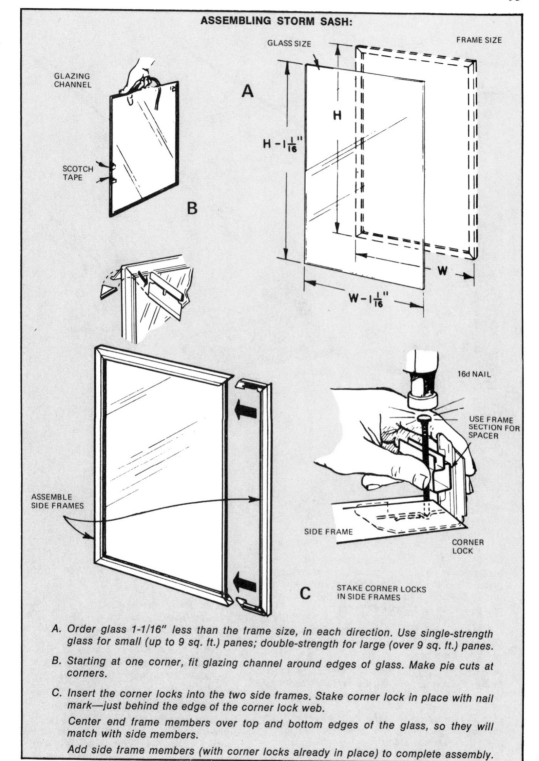

ASSEMBLING STORM SASH:

GLAZING CHANNEL

SCOTCH TAPE

A

B

GLASS SIZE

FRAME SIZE

H

$H - 1\frac{1}{16}''$

$W - 1\frac{1}{16}''$

W

16d NAIL

USE FRAME SECTION FOR SPACER

SIDE FRAME

CORNER LOCK

ASSEMBLE SIDE FRAMES

C STAKE CORNER LOCKS IN SIDE FRAMES

A. Order glass 1-1/16" less than the frame size, in each direction. Use single-strength glass for small (up to 9 sq. ft.) panes; double-strength for large (over 9 sq. ft.) panes.

B. Starting at one corner, fit glazing channel around edges of glass. Make pie cuts at corners.

C. Insert the corner locks into the two side frames. Stake corner lock in place with nail mark—just behind the edge of the corner lock web.

Center end frame members over top and bottom edges of the glass, so they will match with side members.

Add side frame members (with corner locks already in place) to complete assembly.

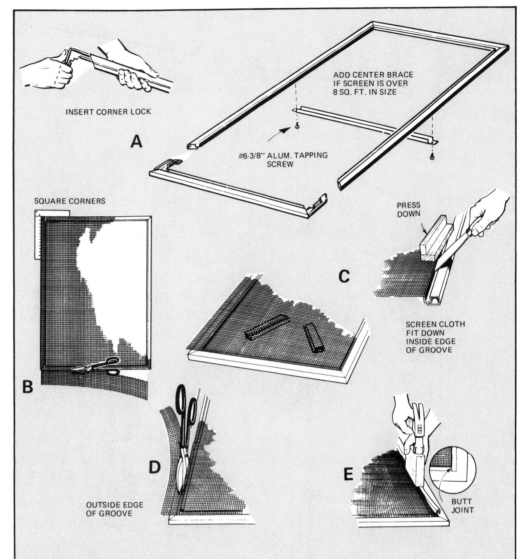

A — INSERT CORNER LOCK — ADD CENTER BRACE IF SCREEN IS OVER 8 SQ. FT. IN SIZE — #6-3/8" ALUM. TAPPING SCREW

B — SQUARE CORNERS

C — PRESS DOWN — SCREEN CLOTH FIT DOWN INSIDE EDGE OF GROOVE

D — OUTSIDE EDGE OF GROOVE

E — BUTT JOINT

A. Insert corner locks into the two short frame pieces. Slip the two long frame pieces onto one of the end pieces. Finally add the other end as shown to complete the frame.

B. Cut screening to outside dimensions of frame. Cut carefully between two screen wires to keep screening square.

Place frame on table and scatter scraps of frame section in the center area to hold screening level with top of frame.

C. Line up screening with the outside edge of the screen groove, at the side and end of the frame shown. Bend the screening into the side and end grooves.

CAUTION: Screening is to fit down inside edge of groove only.

D. After completing operation along one side (as in step above), cut off excess screen cloth along line even with outside edge of groove in other adjacent leg.

E. Cut U-shaped splines to length of spline groove; make butt joints at the corners.

Next, tap spline into groove (on one long frame piece) to hold screening securely.

In the same manner, form screen cloth on the two short sides, cut off excess screen cloth and insert spline. Then, complete fourth side.

A. Screw fasten the jamb hanging brackets into place, 1" in from the side (as shown) and with the back edges against the blind stop.

B. Position the top rail brackets flush with the top of the frame. Punch screw holes in the frame at top of slots with a 4d nail. Attach with sheet metal screws.

C. To install screens or storm windows, angle bottom edge out about 45° to engage top brackets; swing bottom end in.

D. Bottom hooks: Using a 4-penny nail, punch holes close to glass or spline groove 4" from each side. Screw in the hooks. Install the screen or storm window and position the screw eyes so the hooks hold the panel tightly in place.

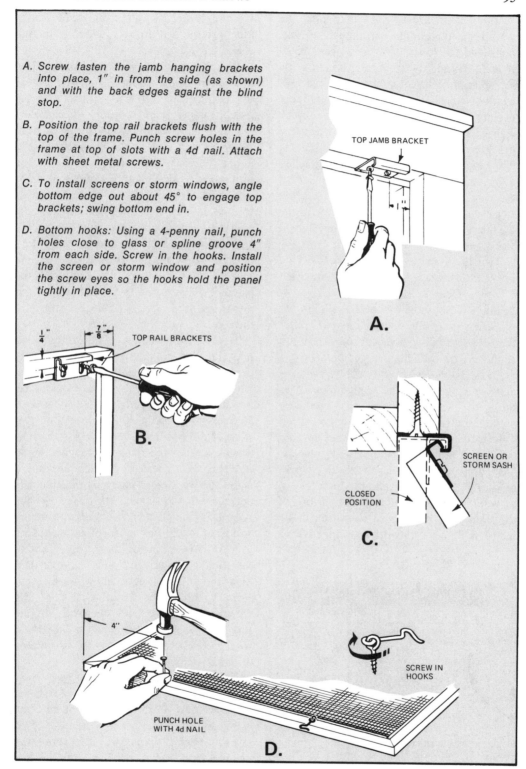

Two screen brackets, used to hold the screen on the window framing, are attached to the top rail of the screen. Place these 3^{15}/$_{16}$-inches from the ends of the screen, and flush with the top of the rail. Mark hole positions at the top of the bracket slots, and punch screw holes in the screen frame using a 4-penny nail. Attach the brackets with ⅜-inch self tapping screws. The other half of each bracket is attached to the window jamb, on the underside of the window casing and 4 inches from the side casings. Put the back edge tight against the blind stop. Fasten in place using ¾ -inch wood screws.

Two hook-and-eye catches are used on the bottom edge of the screen. Place each 4 inches from a lower corner. Use a 4-penny nail to punch pilot holes close to the spline groove to accept the hook. After the screen is hung, locate proper position of the eye on the window framing.

Storm windows. Frames for storm windows are made in the same manner as those for screens, except that you use aluminum framing material shaped a bit differently; it has a glazing channel to hold the glass. Make the frame for a window ⅛-inch shorter than the width and height measurements just outside the blind stops, as before. Check the *outside* dimensions of the frame, and order glass measuring 1^{1}/$_{16}$-inch less than these two frame dimensions.

MATERIALS FOR STORM SASHES	
	Reynolds No.
Aluminum storm sash framing with glazing channel:	
6 ft. lengths	6024
8 ft. lengths	6027
Corner locks (4 per frame)	7210
Hangers (2 units per frame)	7216
Small hooks with screw-eyes (2 each per frame)	
Single- or double-strength glass	

Use single-strength glass for frames up to nine square feet in area, double-strength glass for larger panes.

Fit the flexible glazing channel (removed from the framing material before the metal is cut to frame size) around the glass, starting at one corner. At each corner, snip out a small pie-shaped piece from the front and rear of the channel to form a neat beveled turn. Insert corner locks into the two side (longer) sections of framing, staking them firmly in place with nail-formed indentations just behind the edge of each corner lock web. Now center the shorter frame sections onto the top and bottom edges of the glass, then add the longer side members to complete the assembly. The same types of hangers and hooks as used with screens are added to the top and bottom edges.

Half screens. You can save money on materials by making screens to fit only the lower halves of standard double-hung windows. You make the screen as before, but mount it differently. Install lengths of aluminum *channel* as sliding tracks on two sides of the window frame. Drill and countersink screw holes every six inches along the channel to accept ¾-inch aluminum wood screws. Before fastening the channels permanently in place, try inserting the screen. You will then see just how much you must notch out the top of each channel to permit insertion of the screen. *Important:* make the screen frame ³/$_{16}$-inch less than the opening between window blind stops to allow for the thickness of the channel. Insertion and removal of the screen is easier if the channel is lubricated with products available at gasoline stations or hardware dealers.

Basement windows. A storm sash and/ or screen is fitted on the inside of a basement window if the window opens outward, and on the outside in the case of an inward-opening window. Measure the opening inside the window frame, then

How to Make Screens and Storm Windows

➤ Join adjacent screen frame members by simply pushing them on angular corner locks. Deburr the cut ends before joining them.

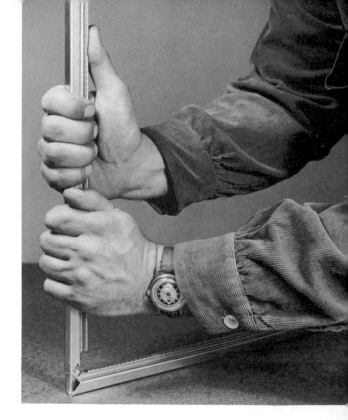

▲ Make a 90-degree corner jig by nailing two strips of $1/4$-inch thick plywood on working surface. This will improve accuracy and lighten your work load.

➤ Screens greater than six square feet in area require cross braces. Use a framing section notched back $5/8$-inch from each end and fastened to the frame as shown. The brace is attached on the back of the frame. Add the brace before the screening is installed, and do not fasten the screening to the brace.

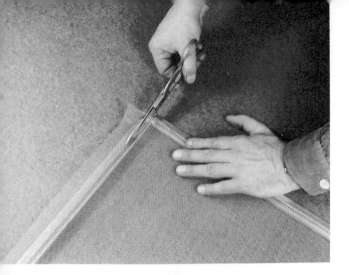

◄ Align selvedged side of screening so that it just covers one long groove. Cut about two inches along the adjacent side and snip off a little of the corner so the screening will fold into the grooves without bunching. Cutting can be done with kitchen shears.

◄ Press screening into groove with a putty knife so that it runs close to the bottom of the groove, but no further. Strips of wood 1/4-inch thick laid under and on top of the screening make it easy to fold neat 90-degree bends in the screening.

◄ Spline locks screening into groove. Hammer a 1/4-inch thick length of plywood laid over the spline to drive it home. Round the edges of the plywood slightly to prevent it from marring the spline. Note that the spline is straight cut, not beveled.

How to Make Screens and Storm Windows

➤ Punch screw holes for screen brackets with a 4-penny nail, then attach the bracket with 3/8-inch self-tapping screws.

▲ Small hooks on bottom rail of screen engage with screw eyes fastened to window frame to hold screen in place. Screw the hooks into pilot holes made with a 4-penny nail.

◀ Jamb brackets on underside of window casing engage screen brackets. They are attached with 3/4-inch wood screws.

add ¾-inch to each dimension to provide a ⅜-inch overlap on all four sides of a *wooden* basement window frame. If you have metal window frames, they probably have holes for attaching screens or storm sash. Use self-tapping screws and clips made from 1 x 1 x 1/16-inch aluminum angle iron to install the storm sash on metal frames. Use round-head wood screws on wood window frames. Attach a strip of felt or rubber tape weather stripping around the edge of the storm sash between the sash and metal window frame. Frames for metal basement windows are made in the same manner as those used for casement windows.

Casement windows. Determine the width of a casement window storm sash by measuring between screw holes you will probably find on the sides of the window frame. For height, measure from top of the crank mechanism to the top of the window frame, then add ¼-inch for overlap at the top. The completed storm sash, or screen, is held in place with angle clips made from 1 x 1 x 1/16-inch aluminum angles. Use self-tapping screws to fasten these to the edges of the frame. Be sure to use felt or rubber stripping between the screen or storm sash frame and a *metal* window frame to prevent accelera-

tion of corrosion that occurs when dissimilar metals are in contact.

Awning windows. If your awning window opens outward, fit the storm sash or screen around the blind stop on the inside. It may be necessary to fit a wood filler strip on the window sill to clear the crank. Drill a hole through the wood for the crank.

Measure the width of the window opening just inside the blind stop and cut the top and bottom sections of the frame ⅛-inch shorter than this dimension. Measure the height from the top of the wood filler strip to the top of the window opening, just inside the blind stop. Make the side pieces of the frame ⅛-inch shorter than this measurement. Attach a strip of felt or rubber weather stripping along the bottom of the sash. Attach the sash or screen with screws passing through the side sections of the frame into the blind stop.

One final tip: measure the width of your window opening at three different positions (top, middle and bottom) and use the shortest dimension if there are differences. Also measure the vertical distance on both sides of the window to be sure that they are the same.   J.H.

See also: GLASS; SCREENS; STORM DOORS AND WINDOWS; WINDOW; WINDOW REPAIR; WINDOWS.

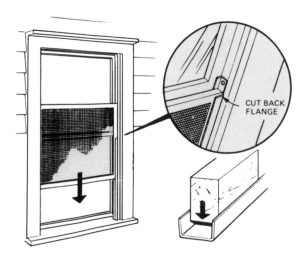

CUT BACK
FLANGE

◄ *Half screens for standard double hung windows may be installed using aluminum channel (Item #6010) as a sliding track. Drill and countersink screw holes every 6" along channel on ³/₄" aluminum wood screws. Cut back flange on one side to insert screen. Spread track slightly if necessary. Attach channel to blind stop flush with the inner edge. Make screen frame 3/16" less than opening between blind stops. Lubricate channel with products available at gasoline stations or hardware dealers.*

How to Make Screens and Storm Windows

▶Casement windows usually have screw holes drilled along sides of frame for installing screens or storm sash on the inside. Measure for width of storm sash between inside edges of holes at sides. For height, measure from top of crank mechanism to frame at top (see sketch). Add 1/4" for overlap at top. Hold completed sash in place with angle clips (made from 1"x1"x1/16" aluminum angle) and self-tapping screws. Whenever aluminum storm sash is installed on a metal frame, be sure to use a felt or rubber strip between them.

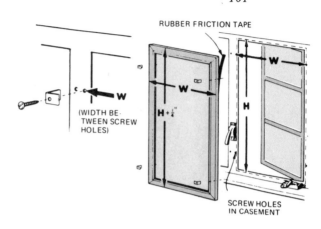

▶Awning windows which open out are fitted with storm sash or screens around the blind stop on the inside of the house. Usually it is necessary to fit a wood filler strip on window sill to clear the crank. Drill a hole through the wood for the crank.

Measure width (W) of opening just inside of the blind stop and cut the top and bottom sections 1/8" less than W. Measure height (H) from top of wood strip to top of opening just inside blind stop. Length of side pieces equal H minus 1/8". Attach a strip of felt or rubber along the bottom of sash. Attach sash or screens with screws through the side sections into blind stop.

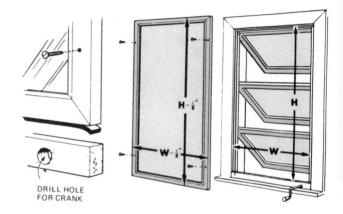

▶Basement windows are fitted with storm sash outside if they open inward or inside if they open outward. Measure the opening inside the window frame. Add 3/4" to height and width for a 3/8" overlap on all four sides of wood frames. For metal frames follow instructions on casement windows. Holes are usually provided in metal window frames for attaching screens or storm sash. Use self-tapping screws and clips made from 1"x1"x1/16" aluminum angle to install the storm sash on metal frames or round head wood screws on wood window frames. Attach a strip of weather stripping, felt or rubber tape, around the edge of the storm sash between the sash and metal window frames.

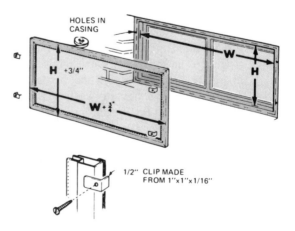

Maintaining Your Aluminum Boat

That hull is tough and corrosion-resistant, but choose an antifouling paint with care

RECENTLY a man said that he wouldn't have an aluminum boat because they just wouldn't hold up in his area. Not too long ago he said the same thing about fiberglass boats and plywood boats. His father swore that the auto was just a passing fad, and that the Wright brothers would never get off the ground.

Of course, aluminum boats got a bad reputation in the early post World War II days when a lot of unknowing—or uncaring—builders bought up surplus aircraft aluminum and turned it into boats. The aircraft alloy contains copper; in salt water, the aluminum in the alloy, being less noble than copper, erodes.

Now, the alloys developed for marine use will last indefinitely in salt water. These alloys are the only ones that the major aluminum producers will furnish to a boat builder, and they are the same as the alloys used in many outboard motor parts. Of course, the surface of unpainted aluminum will corrode. The bright, silver finish turns greyish when it oxidizes. This surface corrosion inhibits further corrosion, however, and has no effect on the durability of the metal.

If a boat is car-topped or trailered to the water for each use, there's no need for a paint job to protect the metal. If the boat is to be kept in the water for any length of time, the bottom should be painted to inhibit marine growth and other fouling. This is true of any boat made of any material.

The secret in providing a good, long-lasting paint job on aluminum is to provide a clean surface. Use a solvent wash of the ordinary petroleum type, an inhibited alkaline cleaner, or an alcohol-phosphoric acid cleaner.

Once the surface is clean, you can apply your paint. Many marine paints available for topside or antifouling use can be applied directly to the metal; for others, a priming coat of zinc chromate is needed.

While it is possible to use a copper-bearing antifouling paint on aluminum, this paint must be applied over a heavy coating of zinc chromate in order to prevent galvanic corrosion, which would result from copper and aluminum in contact whenever the paint is scraped or damaged so the aluminum is exposed to the water. Aluminum producers now discourage the use of copper-bearing antifoulants.

Another type of bottom paint that must not be used is the mercury-bearing type, as the mercury forms an amalgam that will destroy the aluminum.

The tributyl tin oxide antifouling paints have been used most successfully with aluminum. The TBTO paints do not react with aluminum in any way, and they are available in hard racing finishes and soft leaching finishes from most major marine-paint manufacturers. If this paint is scratched so that bare aluminum is exposed, the leaching action continues to provide a measure of protection to the exposed metal.

If an aluminum boat strikes a sub-merged object with considerable force, the metal isn't likely to rupture. Samples were subjected to impact testing of an informal nature—a .38 Police Special revolver bullet at eight feet—and the metal was not punctured.

Of course, it is possible for an aluminum hull to be punctured or torn open by a hard, sharp underwater object; the same is true of boats made of other materials. Fortunately, aluminum boats now offered have built-in flotation, in the form of Styrofoam or polyurethane foam, so the boats will not sink if holed or swamped.

Small abrasions and dents can be repaired by gently hammering the surface to flatten it as much as possible. Any remaining depressions can be filled with epoxy putty after they have been cleaned thoroughly with one of the compounds mentioned above in connection with painting.

If you are handy with tools and are not too concerned with appearance, you can put an aluminum patch over a hole. The patch should extend at least two inches on each side of the hole or rip, and it should be riveted around its perimeter with rivets spaced about one inch apart. Bed the patch in sealant before riveting.

If damage is major and welding is needed, the boat should be returned to the manufacturer or to a welder known to be expert with aluminum Marine aluminum alloys are heat tempered. Too much heat in the area of a weld destroys the temper and leaves the metal brittle. Any flexing at or along the weld could then crack the hull.

No single material is best for all boats; all materials have their advantages and limitations. Whether a boat is good or bad depends on design and the quality of construction. It doesn't make sense to reject a good material on the basis of what was true in a few cases years ago.   T.B.

See also: BOATING; MAINTENANCE, BOAT; PAINTING; PAINT.

How to Erect a Rooftop Antenna

Putting an antenna on your roof is easier than it looks, and it can give your TV set and FM radio a sharp boost in performance

Don't let anyone pressure you into sinking a lot of money into a mile-high mast antenna that may blow down in a storm. And don't think that an antenna is too tough a job to handle yourself. There's no need to hire a high-priced workman to do a job you can do yourself by following the guidelines shown here. A solidly installed rooftop antenna will let you sleep at night without worrying about high winds, and you'll feel better in the pocketbook.

So when you decide it's time for a new or stronger antenna, do the job yourself. A good quality antenna, when installed the do-it-yourself way, will cost less than the cheapest model installed by a "pro." This is one of the repair jobs that the man of the house can handle.

Start off with a good roof (good shingles and joists), a few tools, and the roof mounting antenna. The antenna you buy will probably come with a pretty good mounting base; but for a top-notch, really wind-resistant job, spend a few extra dollars for a small antenna tower. The one shown here cost a little over seven dollars.

With screwdriver, pliers, and crescent wrench in hand, all you do is select the right tower for your particular receiving area. This depends on the kind of signals you wish to receive (UHF, VHF, FM, etc.), distance from the transmitter, and the obstructions in between. Your local TV shop will probably give you pretty good advice on just what kind of antenna and tower you need.

Here to stay. A rooftop tower has many advantages over a mast. It's easier to install, it has a much better appearance, it's more secure, and you eliminate vibrating guy wires that run endlessly from the mast to your house. Very few rooftop antennas blow over during severe storms, so they prevent additional damage to your roof. Should the boom or any of the elements be damaged they can be reached with no trouble at all.

Only a few holes are needed to install the tower on your roof. Before you get started, check and make sure that your antenna will be no higher than other installations in your neighborhood. If necessary, check the local city ordinance for TV antenna installations. Some cities have very exact requirements and even a permit fee. Better to be safe now than sorry later.

Small TV towers come in lengths of 18, 30 and 36 inches, as well as 5- and 10-foot lengths. While they are sturdy and cost little, a tower mounted on a 1½ to 2 story home should provide adequate reception even in a fringe area. If you're really out in the cold, a hi-gain Yagi-type antenna will help to put you in the ball park.

Selecting a site. Once on the roof, select a likely spot for a three-legged tower. We'll help you out by recommending dead center on the roof peak (you get a ground-plane effect this way that will help reduce local r.f. interference somewhat); just count the total number of shingles and divide by two to reach *ground zero.* Mounting the antenna to one side of the roof is possible, but less effective.

Make sure you're clear of tree limbs, etc., and in the line of sight of some TV stations. At all cost, keep away from power lines of any description.

In an extreme fringe area you can mount the tower on the highest part of your roof. But if you've got more than 10 ft. of antenna skyward (extending above the tower), it will have to be guyed properly. Under normal circumstances, however, guy wires shouldn't be necessary. A good rule of thumb is: a five-foot mast extended out of a 30- to 36-inch tower; a

10-foot mast extended out of a 5- to 10-foot tower.

If you're mounting the tower on a flat surface (with no peak), simply center it by using the roof corners as a guide. A friend can hold the boom at approximate dead center while you take sightings from alternate corners.

Mounting tower and mast. Before securing the three-legged tower, check that all three legs are located *over* a roof joist (i. e. supporting beam). The towers have adjustable legs and hold-down feet so this is possible. You can locate the joist by tapping lightly over the surface of the roof.

ʌ*Brush roofing compound on screw heads and bases of stand-offs to seal roof against water penetration.*

◄*Use long screws to attach tripod feet to roof joists. Note that mast is clamped into two rings. Each ring has three locking bolts so that mast can be adjusted to precisely vertical position.*

The first solid thump indicates you've got a beam where you need it.

Temporarily place the legs of the tower on the corresponding joists. Place the two adjoining legs (i.e. the two that form the base of the triangle) in the direction where winds are strongest. It's usually north winds or northwesterlies that cause most problems, but it pays to make sure for your particular area.

Level the tower before securing (lagging) to the joists. A carpenter's level will prove to be a worthwhile investment, but should one be lacking, place the boom (or even the free mast) on the tower and sight it against house outlines and other reference points. When using a level, level the tower and mast in two opposite directions.

Now you can secure the legs to the joists using the supplied screws. Be sure to place at least two screws in the base of each supporting leg. If they don't go directly into the joist you will have to sound out the joist's location again. Probably a shift of ¼-inch is all that will be needed. Make sure that all screws are flush with the tower feet and as tight as possible.

If your combined tower and mast is short enough so that you can reach near the top of the mast, install the mast first so that it is perfectly perpendicular, then clamp on the antenna. If your tower plus mast is too high, fasten the mast to the tower long enough to plumb it, then loosen only one screw in each clamp just enough to free the mast. Attach the mast to the antenna, and remount as a unit.

Antenna up and away. Remove the antenna from the packing carton and prepare it for mounting. Most TV antennas can be unfolded in minutes because the antenna rods lock into position automatically. Simply push or pull the elements into the correct configuration and snap them in place. You'll find it easier to assemble the antenna on the roof, if you have a *flat* roof. If you have a pitched roof, prepare the antenna on the ground and hoist it up with a length of clothesline. Then, if you drop a nut or washer, it can't go rolling into the rain gutter. More important, you won't lunge for a sliding part and end up in the gutter yourself.

If you have a fairly complicated antenna, like the one shown here, you can work with it more comfortably if you screw the support base that comes with the antenna to a scrap of plywood and mount the antenna on the mast. You can move it about easily, study its space requirements (it's a biggie, measuring almost 14 feet!), and make the lead-in wire connections on the ground. As we said before, the base that comes with this antenna is fairly good, and it can be attached to the roof many different ways—on a flat roof, on the side or peak of a pitched roof, or on the eave of a pitched roof. But as we also said, you get a *better* job if you opt for a heavy-duty tower.

To connect the 300-ohm lead-in wire to the assembled antenna, use either small eyelet connectors or form an eyelet with the bare wire. Place the lead tip under a lock washer, tighten the wing nut, and place some electrical tape over the antenna terminals. This will insulate the antenna connections from corrosion due to wind and moisture. Before making the terminal connections, take care to thread the lead-in wire through rubber or other strain-relief devices you may find on the antenna.

If your antenna has a fairly long boom, two brace supports angled from the boom to the mast will add strength. The antenna shown here has an extra boom brace that clamps to the mast and runs parallel with the antenna boom, so no extra braces are needed. Place standoffs on the mast to keep the lead-in cable taut and away from the mast.

If you live close to the transmitters of the channels you want to receive, a relatively simple and inexpensive antenna will suffice. If you live in fringe area, a more elaborate antenna is worth the extra price. This is especially true if you want to pick up UHF channels, which are much harder to pull in than VHF channels. You can buy separate VHF and UHF antennas and mount them one atop the other on the same mast. Or you can obtain a combination antenna that is designed to pull in both VHF and UHF, plus FM radio signals.

The antenna used to illustrate this article is a good example of a combination antenna. It has 39 elements and a boom length of 163 inches. The maximum ranges in miles are: VHF, 185; UHF, 90; FM, 100 miles. A signal lead-in cable brings the signals down into the house. To obtain maximum signal strength, the antenna must be pointed in the direction of the transmitters; if the antenna is even a few degrees off target, TV picture quality can suffer. The easiest way to determine the proper orientation is to tune in various TV channels and have someone evaluate the picture quality as you slowly rotate the antenna mast.

If you have separate VHF and UHF antennas, and perhaps a third antenna for your FM radio, you will need separate lead-ins for each. If you have a combination antenna, the same lead-in does all the work. Just be sure to follow the manufacturer's instructions, and use the hardware provided (cable standoffs, for example) to lead the cable down along the mast and along the rooftop to the point where it enters the house. The cable should be reasonably taut to prevent flopping around in a strong wind, but not so tight that strain is put on connecting points. Standoffs are especially important if you use a conventional twin-lead cable (the flat kind); if you use the more expensive coax cable (round type with shield) to cut down pickup of interfering signals from the local

▲ *Use carpenter's level to make sure mast is vertical. If mast is short, you can install it before putting on the antenna. If the top is out of reach, place antenna on top of mast before placing mast in tripod.*

▼ *Screw the base that comes with the antenna to a piece of plywood. This will hold antenna while you are working on it. The base can be used to mount the antenna on the roof, but a tripod tower is recommended.*

environment, the cable can be taped to the mast. The flat, twin lead should be twisted into a loose spiral, not laid flat, to help cancel unwanted signals generated in the lead-in.

If the lead-in must run along the roof (this would not be necessary if you mount the rig at a gable), use standoffs about every four feet to keep the cable from touching the roof surface. After the tower legs and standoffs are in place, smear roofing cement on screws and around the bases of the standoffs to prevent water leaks.

Bring the antenna lead down the side of the house, again using standoffs every few feet. Try to keep the cable away from metal rain gutters and downspouts, power lines and other obstructions. Bring the cable into the house through a window, or through siding using an insulating ceramic tube. Waterproof this installation also.

Where the lead-in reaches your TV set, you will add a signal splitter that separates the VHF, UHF and FM radio signals so that they can be directed to the proper terminals on the TV set and to the radio equipment. The splitter will probably be part of the antenna package, and the simple installation directions are included.

Do you need an antenna rotator? If all the TV channels you can reasonably hope to pick up are pretty much in the same compass direction from your home, you probably wouldn't have much use for an antenna rotator. But turning the entire antenna system full circle by remote control from your living room is a definite boon if the transmitters of desired TV stations lie in distinctly different directions. Also, a rotating antenna will help you bring in many more distant FM radio stations, if the antenna is also used to pick up radio signals. You may also find that even when TV channels come pretty much from the same direction, a slight off-target orientation of the antenna can help clear

up fuzzy pictures resulting from temporary atmospheric or other signal-messing interferences.

The rotator you buy will include full directions for installation. The kit will include a motor housing you install between the tower and the antenna mast, a low-voltage power cable having from 4 to 8 leads, and a control unit to place near your TV set. The power cable is coded so that you should have no difficulty making the proper terminal connections at both ends. Use more standoffs to lead the cable along the roof and down the side of the house.

Be sure to leave a 1½- to 2-foot loop in the *antenna lead-in* (not the rotator power cable) where it passes the rotator. This loop slack is necessary to prevent binding of the antenna lead-in when the mast turns. Use a standoff above and below the rotator to help keep the antenna lead-in clear. Place the lower standoff in position before you tape the rotator power cable to the mast so that the standoff clamp doesn't cut into the thin insulation of the power cable and cause a short circuit.

Rotator mechanisms have either a north or south starting position. Check the manufacturer's directions for setting the proper starting position. Before you leave the roof, have someone operate the rotator from your living room as you watch to see that all cables are free from possible binding.

This completes your antenna installation. *Almost!* There's just one more thing to do. Add a good lightning arrester with a proper earth ground! You have spent a good deal of money on your new antenna rig, not to mention the hundreds you have sunk into that color TV set; so why risk ruining everything, including your home, by neglecting the installation of a good but very inexpensive ground wire? Your dealer can provide the necessary items, plus complete installation directions. J.H.

How to Erect a Rooftop Antenna

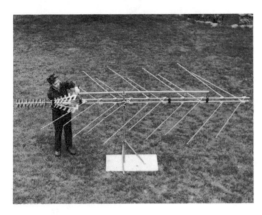 

▲ Unfold antenna elements and assemble them. It is easier to do this job on the roof, if it is flat. If the roof is pitched, assemble the antenna on the ground and pull it up with a length of clothes line (top left).

Make lead-in connections before mounting the antenna. Waterproof the connections and make sure the lead-in cable passes through the flexible strain relief tabs. These are the black tabs sticking down from the boom (top right).

Clamp the antenna to the boom and spray all nuts and bolts with a rust preventive to protect them from corrosion. Note how lead-in passes through strain relief tab at left (above left).

Use stand-offs along mast, rooftop and wall to keep lead-in cable away from house structure. Pull the cable taut, so it won't flap in a wind, but not tightly enough to strain connections (above right).

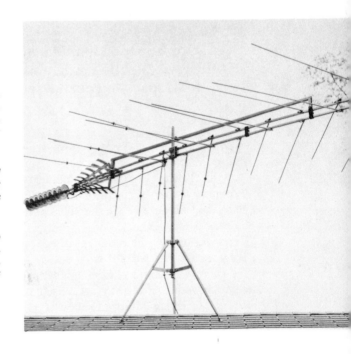

The rooftop antenna in place (at right.) ➤

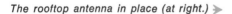

Receiver for Satellite TV Signals

A dish-shaped terminal in the yard can bring programs from space to your TV set

A LANDMARK IN TELEVISION programming was the launching in 1962 of the satellite Telstar. For the first time, television transmissions could be relayed via satellite, and because of Telstar television will never be the same.

Every day of the year, hundreds of hours of programming are beamed from one part of the country to another. Communication satellites hovering in the sky act as signal "mirrors," receiving a transmission and rebroadcasting it back for the world to see.

These space-borne signals can be received by anyone, anywhere. All it takes is a "television receive only" (TVRO) terminal. With such a satellite antenna in your backyard, you can view non-stop sports, news, specials, even first-run movies.

However, putting up a TVRO (or "dish") is more complex than installing a regular television antenna. It takes specialized tools, training, and know-how. At the same time, there are plenty of facts and figures that you should know so you can make an informed decision as to which satellite system is best for you.

How satellites changed TV. Program suppliers always suffered when it came to transporting their shows from place to place. Copies needed to be made; shipping

Receiver for Satellite TV Signals

► *Satellite TV signals originate at uplink transmitters, which send signals to satellites in 5.9 to 6.4 GHz frequency band. Converted signal is sent back to earth in 3.7 to 4.2 GHz band with 5 watts of peak power. Parabolic antenna gathers and focuses signal on electronic feed assembly, which couples it to the LNC. LNC converts signal to UHF frequencies, which go to home receiver. There channel is detected; video and audio are separated for TV viewing.*

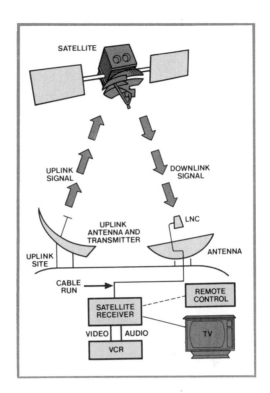

schedules needed to be met; long distribution lists needed to be maintained. All in all, it was an unprofitable and restrictive way to do business. Because technological advancements over recent years have made communications links via satellite easy and cheap, networks and program suppliers were quick to go into space and are now reaping the benefits of having a giant broadcast antenna in the sky.

By all indications, nearly all of the programming seen on television will soon be relayed back and forth via satellites—called "birds" by those in the field—and much of it already is.

Communication satellites used for television broadcasting are stationed in a thin belt 23,300 miles above the equator. Spaced about 350 miles apart from one another, each "looks" at the same portion of the earth all day, 365 days a year. The spacecraft's orbit is called "geosynchronous," that is, one revolution of the satellite is equal to one revolution of the earth—the satellite is always in the same relative position in the sky, allowing us to have continuous satellite broadcasting.

There are currently about a dozen satellites that are used for TV serving the United States. Each one of them has the capacity of 12 channels (some even have 24 channels). So the number of possible programming choices is not difficult to imagine. In fact, most TVRO owners today can tune to 50 or more channels at any time; and each channel is crystal clear.

Make-up of a TVRO terminal. The signal beamed from the satellite is fragile compared to the brutish power belched from regular TV broadcasters. A large parabolic or spherical dish-shaped antenna is used to capture as much as possible of this weak signal. The design of the dish is such that it reflects the "caught" signals to one common point.

At that point is a low noise amplifier, commonly referred to as an LNA. It is a combination signal pick-up device and amplifier. LNAs boost the faint whisperings of a satellite over 100,000 times, and accomplish this amplification while operating at frequencies of billions of cycles per second. TVROs operate at the 4 gigahertz (GHz) microwave range.

The amplified signal is then routed via a special cable to a satellite receiver. This device can tune to any one of the 12 satellite channels. The output of the receiver then connects to the antenna terminals of your television set. Turn the set on and witness a marvelous display of electronic imagery that has gone a long way to come into your living room.

◄ *Heathkit satellite receiver is suitable for home display. Unit is walnut and has built-in memory between preselected channels.*

Let's take a closer look at what is really needed to get a good satellite picture. The dish itself is usually made of fiberglass or metal, and weighs in the neighborhood of 100 to 400 pounds. The most popular dish style used today is parabola shaped. Spherical antennas exist, but they are normally harder to manage. TVRO dishes come in several popular sizes ranging from 10 to 15 feet in diameter. Twelve-footers are a fair average for most applications. The larger the dish, the more signal it can capture and the sharper the picture can be.

The performance of a dish goes way beyond size, however, as not all satellite antennas have the same capability. When choosing a good dish, you will need to give particular attention to the G/T ("gee over tee") ratio, which is its measure of gain over noise temperature. The gain, which is the amplification ability, is expressed in decibels (dB); the noise, which is the amount of "thermal noise" present in the system, is expressed in degrees Kelvin (°K). The higher the G/T, the better.

A heavy-duty, adjustable mount is needed that will not only give the dish proper support, but one that will allow easy realignment. Since the direction of the dish itself must change whenever you wish to look at another satellite, there must be some way to alter its position. Mounts can be either manual or motorized. The mount will need to be anchored to the ground and often will require a solid concrete foundation.

If you have someone else install the dish for you, you can at least save a bit of money by pouring the concrete yourself. A pad three or four feet square by a couple of inches thick will normally be all that is required. Exact measurements will depend on the type and style of mount used.

Many beginning TVRO enthusiasts mistakenly give the matter of solid dish support a quick brush-off. Because of the parachute shape of the dish, hefty winds can produce up to a 3000-pound force on it and sufficient support is vital. Do not try to mount the dish on the roof of your house, unless you absolutely have to. If you do, consult a competent structural engineer first.

The LNA is secured on a tripod or pole-shaped mount that is attached to the front

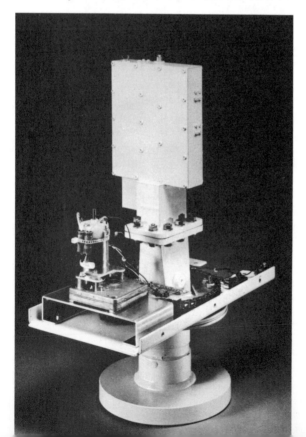

◄ *This is an LNC, a low noise amplifier (LNA) with a down converter built in. LNA picks up and amplifies signals caught by antenna.*

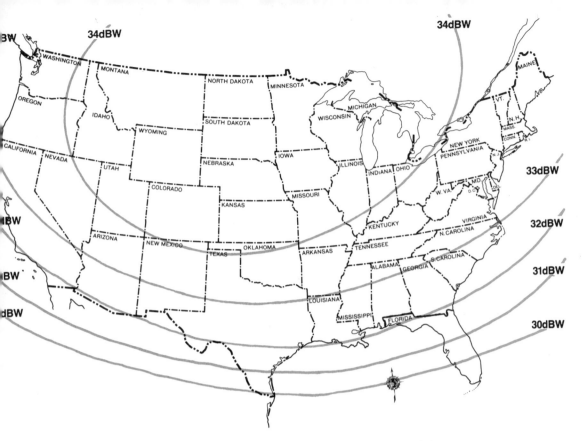

Satellites are so high above the earth that they cover a much larger area than a TV station could. This also means only a tiny part of the original signal will reach any one spot on earth and signals are stronger in some areas than others. The larger the number of contour loops, the better the signal. The one here is relatively weak—loops are large.

side of the dish and is placed at the exact focal point of the antenna. Just as with trying to focus the sun's rays with a magnifying glass, a misplaced LNA will tend to create fuzzy pictures.

Because of a technique known as "opposite sense polarization," some of the satellites can transmit up to 24 broadcasts while using only 12 channels. This is accomplished by getting double usage of the same frequency.

The technique works like this. Radio waves, like light waves, travel both horizontally and vertically; that is, the waves can either be fluctuating up and down or from side to side. A receiving antenna can be designed and installed in such a way that it will accept only one polarization (direction) at a time. An LNA does just that. In one position, it might receive just

the horizontally polarized signals. Rotate the entire unit 90° and it picks up just the vertically polarized signals.

LNAs can be rotated by motorized remote control, or you can accomplish the same function by using what is known as an "orthomode coupler," which makes it possible to use two LNAs on one dish. One is mounted to receive just H signals, the other V signals. In addition, electronic polarization rotators have also been recently introduced to the market.

The cabling used in bringing the signal from the LNA to the indoor receiver is a specially made coaxial type, somewhat similar in design to the kind used in ham, CB, and TV antenna hook-ups. But since satellite transmissions are at the 4 GHz range, the signal has a difficult time getting from one end of a cable to the other (the higher the frequency, the more loss encountered). So, the shorter the cable run, the better. In most home TVRO installations, the typical distance from the dish site to the receiver will be 50 to 200 feet. Longer runs may require a more expensive type of cable known as heliax.

The satellite receiver takes the ultra-high signal, and down-converts it to a usable frequency. It selectively tunes in to any of the 12 common satellite TV frequencies, and then remodulates the signal so it can be fed to your television.

Somewhat new to the home TVRO market is a new breed of LNA and receiver that can make life a bit easier. This LNA has the standard pick-up device and amplifier, but also incorporates a down-converter. The common term for the unit is LNC, for low noise amplifier/down-converter. This device converts the 4 GHz signal to 70 MHz (megahertz, or millions of cycles per second), where regular TV coaxial-type cable can then be used. This type of reception technique is known as "single conversion". A "double conversion" scheme used by some manufacturers involves dropping the 4 GHz signal down to the 700 to 1200 MHz range. This signal is in turn sent to the receiver which then down-converts it again, this time to 70 MHz.

Double conversion equipment, although usually more expensive than the other types, enables you to use more than one receiver with each low noise amplifier. This is particularly useful when members of the house want to watch different programming. You can also erect one dish and share it and the LNC with your neighbor. Each of you would then buy a receiver, and you could both enjoy satellite television for about half of the normal cost.

One important point about LNC/Receiver combos is that unlike regular LNAs and receivers, which allow for interchangeability between brands and models, you must use the LNC with its own receiver.

LNAs and LNCs are usually rated by their thermal noise temperature, which is the amount of background noise generated by the device itself. Common values for LNA/LNCs are 120°K, 100°K, and 85°K. The lower the number, the lower the noise and hence the better the device. The performance of the LNA or LNC is perhaps the single most important factor when choosing a satellite system.

Different areas of the country will need varying qualities of equipment. Most of the satellites look at the entire United States. This satellite "look" area is called a footprint, and the outside edges of this footprint are usually weaker than the central portion. So if you live on the West Coast, or perhaps in the lower southeast, you may need not only a better quality LNA or LNC, but a larger-than-average, good performance dish. You can get a visual picture of a satellite footprint by referring to the illustration on p. 113. The different energy loops of the signal beam are representations of the effective isotropic radiated power (EIRP), and they are stated in "decibels over one watt" (dBW). Typical signal levels may be 35 dBW at the center of the footprint, with levels dropping to under 31 dBW at the edges. The loss of a single dB in a "marginal" TVRO installation can mean the difference between clarity and fuzziness. For more details about what you will need, consult a local TVRO dealer. He will know from experience what your area requires.

Putting up a dish. Several factors need to be considered when deciding on purchasing a satellite system. One of the most important things you should decide is where you will put it.

Since the satellites are positioned over the equator, you will need to tilt the dish towards southern skies. And since the satellites are spaced many degrees apart from one another, and they span a distance from one edge of the country to the other,

▶ Two young men assemble a satellite antenna. Two pairs of adult hands can usually do the job without difficulty.

you will need to swing your dish in a fairly wide arc in order to tune in to all of them. Needless to say, mountains, trees, water towers, even your own house, may shield the signal from your dish. In order to operate properly, the satellite antenna *must* have an unobstructed line of sight to the satellite.

Proximity to your house is important, too. If you have a manual tracking mount, you will need to go outside and crank the dish around each time you want to make contact with a different satellite. Longer cables, especially with the standard non-converting LNAs, can be expensive and can create a great amount of signal loss. Two hundred feet should be the maximum distance for most home TVRO installations. Longer runs will require more complicated and expensive parts.

Another factor in choosing a system and site is "terrestrial interference." The 4 GHz frequencies used in satellite transmissions are the same as those used by land-based microwave systems, such as those operated by a telephone company. If your house is right near a microwave path, you could be in for some interference problems. It always pays to have a site survey performed so you can avoid the headache and financial shock of finding your TVRO cannot be used at your

house. Most reputable TVRO dealers can handle the survey for you.

After the survey is complete, and there are no microwave paths near you, you can help protect your satellite reception interest by licensing your TVRO with the Federal Communications Commission (licensing is purely voluntary). Then, you have the chance to challenge any company who may later wish to construct a microwave link that could pose interference problems.

The next step is to lay the foundation and set up the mount. The dish usually comes in sections—2 to 12 or more—and after assembly, the dish is bolted to the mount. The LNA is then attached to the dish and rough adjustments are made to get the dish in the correct operating position. The cable is then connected between the LNA and the receiver. If all works well, the dish is "fine tuned," which can take two well-trained installers several hours to complete.

When it is found that the dish will "track," that is, swing from one satellite to the other, and the reception is as clear as can be, the installation is complete and the time has come to relax and enjoy your giant ear to the heavens.

With a TVRO, the old familiar expression, "There's nothing on TV" is no longer true. Now, everything is on TV.   G.M.

Pollution Control Systems

Neglect of these devices can lead to
poor performance, increased engine wear

DETROIT'S EFFORT to curb automobile-caused air pollution has spawned a wide assortment of underhood gadgetry.

Examples include positive crankcase ventilation (popularly called PCV), the air injection system, the thermostatically controlled air cleaner, a carburetor solenoid designed to keep the critically tuned engine from running on after it is turned off, and systems that retard ignition timing at low engine speeds ("vacuum choppers").

The first of the antipollution systems was PCV. It was introduced in the early 1960's to replace the road draft tube. With the road draft tube, gasoline fumes in the crankcase were purged to the atmosphere. PCV instead reroutes the fumes from the crankcase back into the engine via the carburetor intake, and from there into the combustion chamber for burning.

The most widely used PCV systems are these: 1) Fresh air is drawn from the air cleaner through a hose into an otherwise closed oil filler cap. The air circulates through the engine, picking up fumes and exhaling them into the PCV valve. The PCV valve regulates the flow of the fumes through a hose into the carburetor air intake (at the carburetor base). Here the fumes mix with the incoming air-fuel charge and go into the combustion chamber for burning. 2) Fresh air is drawn through the filter built into the oil filler cap. This filter usually is made of wire mesh. The air flow through the engine from this point is the same as the first type.

The PCV valve is a spring-loaded device that regulates flow according to manifold vacuum (as vaccum drops, the valve opens further). Clearly, the fumes that flow through the valve deposit soot on its working parts, and the valve in time will plug. The valve in some systems must be replaced once a year, although this interval can be extended by periodic cleaning with an appropriate solvent.

There is more to servicing PCV than replacing the valve, or even cleaning it. The PCV system should be checked at every available opportunity, for on many cars it will need service at least four times a year, and preferably every two months, particularly as the car ages.

The ventilation system does not change with the age of the vehicle, so its maximum capacity for handling crankcase fumes is fixed. But as the engine wears, more and more unburned fuel blows by the piston rings into the crankcase. A worn engine can deposit three to four times as much unburned gasoline into the crankcase. Therefore, it is important to keep the ventilation system clean and operative, to handle the increasing loads imposed by engine wear.

If the system is poorly maintained, the

blow-by fumes will condense in the crankcase and dilute the oil, increasing engine wear. The buildup of pressure in the crankcase from the fumes actually can be sufficient to cause engine oil leaks.

More blow-by also agitates the oil, breaking some of it into droplets, which will mix with the crankcase fumes and be blown out the inlet breather (if the pressure is high enough) or drawn through the PCV valve into the engine. The engine will burn rather large quantities of oil, particularly at higher engine speeds, when blow-by reaches a maximum.

PCV service is also important for two other reasons. 1) Most new car warranties require at least periodic replacement of the PCV valve, and some require frequent checking and cleaning of the valve. 2) The engine is designed to run smoothly with a clean and properly functioning PCV system. If the system malfunctions, the engine performance will be affected; rough idle is one ailment common to engines with malfunctioning PCV.

To check out the two common PCV systems, proceed in this manner. With type 1, run the engine at idle, remove the hose from the air cleaner and place your finger over the hose end. You should feel vacuum. Note: some PVC systems of this type have an additional filter of wire gauze in the end of the hose. If you just try to pull off the hose, without removing the filter first, you will damage the molded end of the hose. Take off the air filter cover, remove the regular element and check for the presence of this gauze filter. If it is there, replace if dirty and refit after checking the entire system.

If you feel vacuum at the end of the hose, proceed directly to the PCV valve. On most cars, it can be pulled out of the rocker cover. Shake the valve and if it rattles, it is all right. Just clean it with special solvent, using the procedure discussed later in this section. If the valve

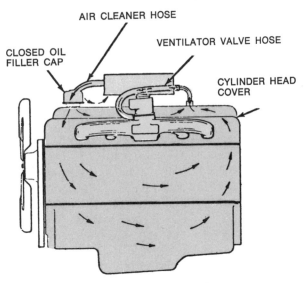

SIX-CYLINDER ENGINES

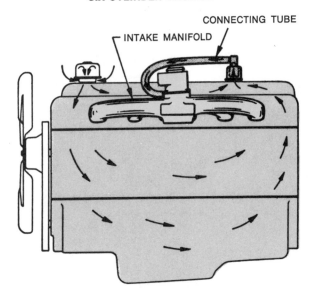

▲ *Above is most common type of PCV system. Fumes are drawn from crankcase into intake manifold for reburning. Below is another type of system. Only difference is that a filter is built into the oil filler cap.*

doesn't rattle, try cleaning it, and if cleaning doesn't work, install a new valve.

If you do not feel vacuum at the end of the hose disconnected from the air cleaner, pull off the oil filler cap, and again run the engine at idle. Place a piece of paper over the oil filler tube and within a few seconds it should be sucked against the tube. If this happens, the hose to the air cleaner is plugged, probably because of contamination from heavy blow-by fumes that are backing up through the system and/or plugging somewhere else in the PCV system. Replace the hose. If the engine is old, there is not much you can do about the cause of this condition except check the PCV system frequently.

Now let's introduce the checking procedure for the type 2 system. Remove the oil filler cap and look at the wire mesh filter. If dirty, clean it in solvent and let it air dry (or blow it dry with compressed air). Then make the same test as with the type 1 system, using the piece of paper over the oil filler tube with the engine idling. From this point, the checking and service procedure for both systems is the same.

If the paper is not sucked against the oil filler tube, disconnect the PCV valve from the rocker cover or engine valley cover (wherever it is mounted). Or if the valve is mounted at the carburetor, disconnect the hose connection at the rocker cover or engine valley cover.

With the engine idling, place your finger over the end of the valve or hose, and you should feel vacuum. If there is none, check the hose for plugging. If the hose is good, remove the valve completely and check for vacuum at the carburetor base. If there is vacuum here, the valve is plugged and must be cleaned or replaced.

If there is no vacuum at the carburetor base, the carburetor vacuum passage is clogged. Remove the carburetor and clean the passage by dunking the lower end in

⋏ *If possible, disconnect hose at air cleaner, run engine and feel for vacuum at end of hose.*

➤ *If there is vacuum at other end of system, check at PCV valve. On most cars, valve sits in grommet in rocker cover. Just pull it out.*

solvent and cleaning the neck with a small drill bit. Select a drill bit that will not remove any metal, and hand turn the bit through the neck. Even if the system checks out, the valve should be cleaned. The best way is with one of the special cans of solvent designed for the job with a tapered spout. Note: unless it is early two-piece design, General Motors recommends replacement rather than cleaning.

With the engine off, disconnect the hose or valve at the rocker cover or engine valley cover (as you did to check for vacuum). By leaving the vacuum side connected (at the carburetor base), the solvent will be drawn through the valve, cleaning it, when you run the engine.

Insert the solvent can spout into the open end of the PCV valve, and work it back and forth against the spring-loaded plunger while squirting a few shots of solvent into the valve interior. If the valve is mounted on the carburetor, and squirting solvent into the hose doesn't clean and free up the valve, disconnect the hose at

With engine running, feel for vacuum at end of PCV valve.

If there is no vacuum at end of PCV valve, place paper tag on oil filler cap neck (cap removed, engine idling). Paper should be sucked against neck and held by crankcase vacuum.

If there is no vacuum anywhere, check hose neck at base of carburetor. If vacuum is weak with engine running, neck may be clogged. Clean with a small drill bit.

the other end and work the solvent in against the spring-loaded plunger.

Now start the engine and let it idle. Squirt a few more shots of solvent into the valve, reconnect it and let the engine run for a few more minutes to evaporate the solvent. PCV puts a tremendous strain on the regular air filter in most PCV systems which have the hose connected to the air cleaner. So check the air filter element frequently as part of your PCV checkout.

Two of the newest anti-pollution systems, exhaust gas recirculation and evaporative emission control, also are among the most widely used.

Virtually all cars since 1971 have been equipped with evaporative emission control. EEC eliminates the vents in the fuel system; when the engine is shut off, fuel vapors that would otherwise evaporate into

and pollute the atmosphere are trapped inside. In the typical EEC design, the vapors are trapped in a charcoal canister. When the engine is started, a valve opens, permitting engine vacuum to suck the vapors out of the canister. The vapors then flow into the cylinders for burning.

All evaporative emission control systems use a gas cap with pressure and vacuum valves to prevent damage to the gas tank, and to permit gasoline to flow. As gasoline is drawn from the tank, a vacuum void is created, which if not filled with air would soon result in cessation of fuel flow. Additionally, the vacuum might cause collapse of the gas tank. To prevent this, the gas cap vacuum valve opens, and air flows in to fill the void. If gasoline expansion creates pressure, the pressure valve opens to relieve it, preventing rupture of the tank. True, the fuel system is vented when either of these valves opens, but when the system has to be closed—when the engine is off—it is.

Service of the evaporative emission control system is limited to checking hoses and connections, and replacing the foam filter in the base of the charcoal canister once a year (see illustration). However, many cars built in 1981 have sealed canisters which must be replaced if faulty or according to maintenance schedules. Always replace a hose with one designed for the EEC system. Another type may be pre-

▲ PCV valve can be cleaned with special solvent, as shown. If solvent fails to free up valve, it should be replaced. Good preventive maintenance practice is to replace valve once a year, and clean with solvent six months later.

➤ Foam filter in base of evaporative emission control charcoal canister is easily pulled out for service.

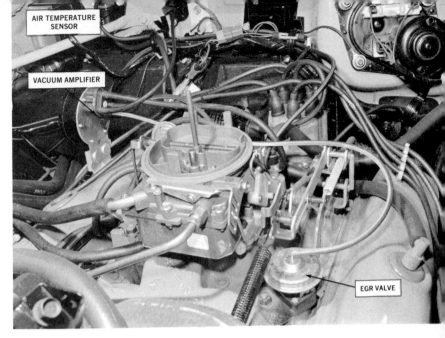

AIR TEMPERATURE SENSOR

VACUUM AMPLIFIER

EGR VALVE

This is one of Chrysler Corp.'s exhaust gas recirculation systems of the type that uses a vacuum amplifier for a vacuum signal from the carburetor Venturi. On most models, a coolant sensor in the radiator top tank is used rather than the air temperature sensor shown here.

maturely deteriorated by the fuel vapors. The correct hose to use has the word "Fuel" imprinted on it.

If you ever replace the gas cap (either because it is lost or to switch to a locking design), be absolutely certain you have a cap designed for the EEC system. Failure to use a cap with pressure relief and vacuum valves not only will defeat the system, but if you mistakenly use a non-vented cap, it would cause the gas tank to collapse. Just because a cap fits the fill neck doesn't mean it is the right type.

The exhaust gas recirculation system first appeared on 1972 California-bound cars, then was installed nationwide in 1973, to control oxides of nitrogen, another major air pollutant. Oxides of nitrogen are formed in the cylinders when combustion temperatures reach peaks. The injection of a small amount of exhaust gas back into the combustion chamber reduces the peak temperatures.

Injection of exhaust gas is regulated on most cars by a vacuum-operated flow control valve, the EGR valve. The vacuum control on the valve is somewhat different from car to car. In one Chrysler Corp. design, the vacuum is tapped off the venturi portion of the carburetor air horn. This provides the control that Chrysler

wants for certain engines, but the vacuum signal is not strong enough to operate the valve. The weak signal is fed into a "vacuum amplifier," which is a mechanical version of a transistor. It works as a form of relay to control a stronger vacuum supply and it is the stronger vacuum supply that actually moves the EGR valve.

Some other Chrysler products have no EGR valve. Instead, calibrated jets permit exhaust gas to flow from the exhaust crossover passage in the intake manifold into the air-fuel passages of the intake manifold, just under the carburetor.

Naturally, the pumping back of some already burned gasoline causes a bit of deterioration in engine performance, so the car manufacturers have designed systems that cut out the exhaust gas recirculation when it might cause problems: at idle, when it could cause engine stalling; at very low outside air temperatures, when it could cause driveway problems; at very high coolant temperatures, when the reduced performance could contribute to overheating; at full throttle, when performance is needed for passing.

The sensors that defeat the system are not used on all cars. Their use varies according to the needs of different engines.

A basic check of the exhaust gas recirculation system should be made as part of a tuneup. On Chrysler products without the valve, remove the air cleaner and hold the choke and throttle plates open. Using a flashlight, inspect the jets through the carburetor air horn; if they are open, all is okay. If not, remove the carburetor, unthread the jets and clean in solvent. Warning: the jets are non-magnetic, so be careful not to let them fall into the intake manifold during removal or reinstallation, for you will not be able to get them out with a magnet. You'll have to pull the intake manifold and shake them out.

On all other cars with the valve, you can make a basic check when ambient air temperature is about 70 degrees or above. Warm up the engine and let it idle. Snap open the throttle to about 2000 rpm and watch the external shaft on the EGR valve. It should move visibly. Repeat the test if necessary to confirm movement, which is slight. If you cannot *see* it move, feel for movement—but wear a glove. If there is

definitely no movement, either the valve is defective or there is a poor hose connection. All hoses should be checked for looseness and deterioration, and replaced if necessary, as a routine matter. If the valve is defective, the simplest procedure is to replace it, although it theoretically can be cleaned. A defective EGR valve can cause heavy spark-plug knock.

Exhaust gas recirculation systems have a somewhat different effect on each cylinder, so if you wish to check the engine power balance, you must first disconnect the vacuum hose to the valve, and plug the hose end. On Chrysler products with the calibrated jets, you cannot do a power balance test unless you temporarily plug the jets in the intake manifold. Because of the obvious difficulty this entails, compression and vacuum gauge tests would appear to be the only ones you should make prior to tuneup.   P.W.

See also: AIR CLEANERS; ENGINE; PARTS REPLACEMENT, ENGINE.

EGR VALVE

◄ *GM's exhaust gas recirculation system has an easily identifiable valve.*

All about Antiquing

Follow these steps to achieve a professional-looking result on a piece of furniture — whether it's an old relic or brand new

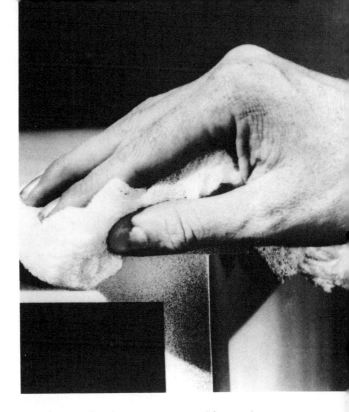

ANTIQUING is definitely "in" the home scene these days and thanks to the magic of the new antiquing kits now available it's possible to make an old piece of furniture that you've had lying around the basement or attic look brand new—or give a new piece you've just purchased the charming appearance of age.

There are several steps you can take to assure a professional-looking result. First of all, be sure to remove all handles, knobs or other hardware as it is far easier to work on a smooth surface. It is not necessary to remove old finishes, varnish or enamel, unless you want to reduce the surface to the bare wood. In that case a paint and varnish remover will do the job.

Cleaning is done by scrubbing all surfaces with tri-sodium phosphate, ammonia and water, or an abrasive household detergent using a small brush—such as a toothbrush—to get into hard-to-reach areas. Wash off all traces of the cleaning agent with clear water and allow the surface to dry.

Sanding. The final results of your antiquing job may depend on whether or not the piece of furniture you are working on is sanded properly. To obtain the best results you should use three different grades of sandpaper, starting with the coarsest of the three, and applying the finishing touches with the finest one. You can make the sanding process—which insures adhesion of the paint—much easier by using a wooden block covered with the sandpaper, coarse side out. Any deep cuts or abused areas need not be sanded smooth, as they will absorb more of the toner, producing a "distressed" effect.

If you want to fill any scratches or mars, a plastic wood filler will accomplish this job, and these areas can be sanded smooth after thoroughly dried. If you wish, these fillers can be colored to match the natural wood tones of the furniture and chalk like color mixtures can be bought with the filler at most stores.

When all sanding is completed, dampen a cloth with mineral spirits, and clear all the surfaces of dust.

Undercoating. Once the piece is dry and clear of all dust you may apply the undercoating. Read the label instructions carefully, making sure that the coating is stirred thoroughly so that there isn't any pigment collected at the bottom of the can.

If you use a spray-gun to apply the paint, you should add two tablespoons of mineral spirits to thin the mixture enough to insure an even flow of paint. Remove all drawers and doors, place them on a flat horizontal surface—to avoid streaking—and you're ready to begin.

Use a flat, wide brush for the larger surfaces, painting one side of the piece of furniture at a time. By applying long, even strokes with the grain of the wood you will produce the best results. For any piece with prominent legs, turn it upside down and paint the legs first, followed by the top and work downward.

Only enough undercoating to cover the surface well should be applied, letting it dry for about twelve or twenty-four hours. Then sand lightly, and you're ready for the toner.

Applying toner. After you have stirred the toner thoroughly with a wooden paddle, read the label instructions carefully, applying a thin coat of the toner in the same manner as suggested for the undercoating. Be sure to pay special attention to any carved trim and crevices, painting them first to allow more absorption of the toner. Let the color toner set for ten to thirty minutes before beginning to rub.

Rubbing. Here you can use your imagination along with a cheese cloth, dry brush and steel wool. Just be sure to step back and check your progress every so often to make sure you aren't overdoing it.

Rub large, flat areas in long, even strokes, starting with a light touch and apply more pressure as you go along. If you discover you've allowed the toner to set too long, simply dampen your rub cloth with mineral spirits. If the reverse is true and you haven't permitted the toner to set long enough, you can apply another coat and wait again.

The difficulty in rubbing intricate carved trim can be overcome by using a cotton tip in those hard-to-reach areas. After rubbing, allow at least twenty-four hours for the paint to dry thoroughly.

If you want to add a protective coat of

▲ *Above: A few wear marks give wood the aged look of antiques. Right: With a propane torch you can flame-finish a piece for further aging. Be sure to keep the torch moving.* ➤

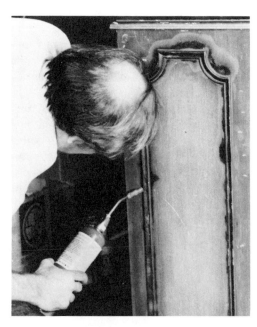

All about Antiquing

clear varnish, it can be applied as soon as the toner has dried. But if you wish to wax the surface, it is best to allow the paint to dry for at least a week before applying.

Special effects. After the coat of toner is applied, there are several methods which can be used to achieve interesting special effects:

Grain. For a wood grain simulation, use a dry brush for your rubbing. Place a small amount of toner on a piece of tin foil or glass, touching the tip of the brush lightly in the color. Apply in long, even strokes, with the grain of the wood but in irregular lines.

Splattern. For this artistic touch use a stiff bristle brush, such as an old tooth-brush. Dip the ends of the brush into the paint, and "spring" the bristles with your finger to throw a fine spray of toner over the undercoated surface. Check the desired effect by practicing on a piece of paper first, remembering that too much toner on the brush could result in splotches.

Water stained wood. This interesting and traditional look is accomplished by first rubbing the toned surface, then splattering it with mineral spirits. The toner spreads out in the spots where the liquid has fallen, creating an authentic water stained look.

Marble. Apply a relatively heavy coat of toner to your surface, then lay a large piece of wrinkled, clear plastic lightly on top of the area. Pat the plastic lightly with a cloth, making sure wrinkles and air bubbles are in evidence. Then pick up the plastic quickly and carefully, but be sure not to drag it. Similar effects can be achieved by using a feather, a sponge or burlap, or a combination of these materials.

Tortoise shell. The best way to create this effect is to work on one small area at a time. Applying a heavier than usual amount of toner glaze, tap the surface lightly with your fingertips, changing the

▲ *Use a wire brush to carefully remove excess char after using propane torch. Charring looks particularly good on moldings.*

angle of your hand each time. A similar effect can be accomplished by tapping the surface with a short bristle brush, beginning in the center of the area and working toward the edges.

Distressed. If your piece of furniture isn't naturally worn, this popular antiquing effect can be simulated. You can make your own scratches and mars simply by beating the surface with a heavy tool, or a burlap bag filled with chains. After sanding the scratches, apply the artists oil paint "raw umber" straight from the tube, rubbing off the excess paint vigorously.

Distressed paint. To achieve this effect you apply two layers of contrasting colors to your furniture, allowing each to dry thoroughly. Using a coarse grade of sand paper, lightly sand the surface until the initial color is in evidence. Do this only in those spots where normal wear would occur.

See also: ABRASIVES; FINISHING, WOOD; FURNITURE, USED; LUMBER; PAINTING.

Trouble-shooting Home Appliances

Here's how to do everything you can, depending on your tools and experience, to head off those costly visits by the repairman

T HERE ARE SEVERAL steps you should consider before deciding what to do when an appliance breaks down or fails to operate in a normal manner. Whenever you are faced with such a situation, check-out the following pre-service program before deciding how to proceed. You may need to go no further to clear up your trouble.

Make certain there is a problem. Have you read the operating instructions supplied with your appliance so well that you are sure you know how to operate it properly and are entirely aware of what the manufacturer claims it will do? If not, read over the instructions carefully. In any case, the steps outlined below will help you spot unusual performance by localizing the problem.

Incorrect use? Maybe the person using your machine did not know how to handle it. Did she (or he) get careless? Did she expect too much? Did she overload the machine?

Is this a new operator who has not been properly instructed in how to use the appliance? (A young member of the family? a visitor? or a maid?) The same type of appliance built by a different manufacturer may have a different load capacity and/or methods of control. A user should be "checked out" on each machine.

External supply failure? An electrical appliance must have electricity, so make certain that there is power to the appliance; that the fuse hasn't blown, and that the plug hasn't pulled out of the socket.

A gas appliance must have gas. Make sure that the valve hasn't been shut off in the gas supply line.

An oil burner must have fuel. Be certain the tank isn't empty.

A water-using appliance must have the water turned on, an adequate supply of water, and the kind of water needed to do the job for which the appliance is designed.

Make certain that the temperature of the water at its points of use is within the range recommended by the manufacturer. For example: Dishwashers require water temperature in the tub within a 140° - 160° range, for each wash and rinse cycle.

You must be sure there is enough water available to operate the appliance. Both water pressure and condition of the supply are important factors and should be considered as a pair. These two control "flow rate" or gallons per minute (gpm). A low flow rate will not allow some appliances time to fill with enough water to do a good job.

Water quality such as pollution, hardness, and iron are important factors. Be sure that clean water is available. Polluted water can be a health hazard. This is unlikely with a public water supply, but you could still have pollution with an improper

Trouble-shooting Home Appliances

plumbing connection. In the country, a well may easily become polluted. If there is any question, have your water analyzed by your local health officer.

Chemical impurities (as opposed to biological pollution) are also major problems. Mineral content such as calcium, iron, etc., will leave deposits on dishes, in clothes, and in the plumbing. Many problems of washability and poor flow are caused by "hard water."

Physical damage? Not a fault of the machine, this concerns damage done to an appliance in normally good condition, free of any failures. Examples are dropping, fire, flood, etc. This is a matter of judgment.

Is your machine worth fixing? Minor damage such as broken handles, dials, knobs, cabinet dents, and scratches should be easy to fix. Individual damaged parts can be ordered and you can replace them.

In case of fire or flood: clean out the machine thoroughly and bake the electrical parts dry at a low temperature (180°), in your oven for several hours. Check all contacts for cleanliness and all insulation for damage. Make sure that all connections are tight and see that all moving parts are operating smoothly.

Make certain that the gear box, crankcase, and such are properly lubricated and free of water and other impurities. Clean all sand, soot, and carbon deposits from all electrical connections and terminals. Remove all rust and protect the surface with a proper finish. Replace any questionable parts.

Operation failure? This is the machine-breakdown situation in which the appliance will not start, has suddenly stopped, or isn't working the way it should. After checking the external factors, you have decided that the trouble is within the appliance. Now you stop, look, listen, smell—and think!

The smell of burning insulation is a warning to turn off or disconnect your machine promptly. Then remove the cover and/or electrical part to check for burned insulation and smoke smudges. Once you find the part, it can be removed and replaced. It is usually less costly to replace burned out electrical parts than to repair them. If the insulation is burned off a connecting wire, the parts connected to this

▼ *Most appliances usually work. If one stops working, check simple things first. Is it being used properly? Is it getting enough water? Is it plugged in?*

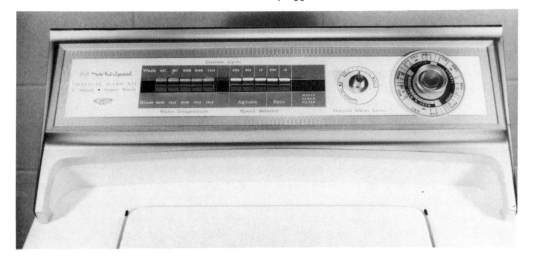

wire must be checked for "shorts" or "grounds."

Listening will tell if there are any unusual squeaks, rattles, bangs, or if your machine is "dead," assuming the switch is on.

If your appliance is inoperative, or partially so, the procedure is to use a volt-ohmmeter to check for a faulty circuit. Follow the electrical supply circuit until you come to a point where there is no reading. This indicates that there's probably something wrong between that point and the one tested just before.

Home appliance repairs. Rattles and similar noises are usually due to something loose that is vibrating or swinging out of place and hitting another part of the machine. You will have to listen and look for the offending part.

Look first for a foreign object such as a bottle cap, button, bobby pin, marble or a coin which may be floating, bouncing, rolling, or caught in a moving part of your machine. Once found, the remedy will suggest itself.

It may only be necessary to tighten some screws. However, the noise may be caused by a worn bearing which would have to be replaced. This is usually a special tool job!

Squeaks are that source of noise made by two surfaces rubbing each other or friction. It may be caused by two loose pieces of metal, which can be tightened. Lack of lubrication has a characteristic sound. Proper use of grease or oil will often remedy such noises. Another cause of noise could be a slipping belt, which usually requires a tension adjustment.

Looking carefully will often reveal a great deal about the condition of your machine. The broken control knobs previously mentioned might be binding against the escutcheon to prevent proper operation.

The door lid on many appliances operates a switch to shut off the machine while it is open. If the door is not closed tightly the machine will not start. A slight push to secure the latch may be all that is needed; however, a simple hinge or latch adjustment may be required.

A loose drive belt can be tightened; all machines have an adjustment for that. On some there is automatic tension adjustment; on others it is manual. This is usually evidenced by slow or erratic operating speed.

Keep all appliances clean. An abnormal collection of dust and dirt in a machine will certainly affect its performance. For instance, lint in your dryer can be a hazard; dust on your refrigerator coils will cause it to run too much.

A panel bulb or indicator light may be burned out. Your owner's manual may point out that it should be considered a "safety light," such as with freezers, and that as long as it was lighted everything was fine. So check it before you look further. Even the best bulbs have an end to their life sometime.

Water leakage is self evident. Once the source of a leak is located, replace the hose or tighten the clamp. Pump or tub leaks will require replacement of the part. Patching is *not* a satisfactory permanent repair.

Electrical testing. After you have checked the machine for mechanical problems the next step is to check the electrical system—both wiring and parts.

Electrical wiring and testing. Before trying to locate trouble in the electrical circuitry of an appliance you should know how to read a wiring diagram. This is the electrical map showing which parts are which and how they are connected to each other. There are many signs and symbols with which you will need to become familiar before you will be able to understand a diagram and use it intelligently. The table lists the symbols most commonly used.

APPLIANCE WIRING DIAGRAM SYMBOLS

(Note: S.P.S.T. means single-pole single-throw; S.P.D.T. means single-pole double-throw; N.O. means normally open and N.C. means normally closed.)

MANUAL AND MECHANICAL SWITCHES

S.P.S.T.

S.P.D.T.

S.P.D.T.
(2 Contacts on One Side)

Multi-Position

Push-Button (N.O.)
(Momentary Contact)

Push-Button (N.C.)

Push-Button
(Two-Circuit)

Timer Switch

Pressure Operated
(S.P.D.T.)

Centrifugal Switch

Master or Control Sw.
(Number of Positions
and Internal Contact
Operation as Required)

OFF
HI COOL
MED. COOL
LO COOL
L1 2 3 4 5 L

(TYPICAL EXAMPLE)

TEMPERATURE ACTUATED COMPONENTS

(Note: Symbols shown to be used for thermostats, bimetal switches, overload protectors, or other similar components, as required.)

S.P.S.T.
(Open on Heat Rise)

S.P.S.T.
(Close on Heat Rise)

TEMPERATURE ACTUATED COMPONENTS

(Note: Symbols shown to be used for thermostats, bimetal switches, overload protectors, or other similar components, as required.)

Temp. Actuated
(Close on Heat Rise)

Temp. Actuated
(Open on Heat Rise)

S.P.S.T.
(Open on Heat Rise)

S.P.D.T.

S.P.D.T.

S.P.S.T.
(Two Contacts)

S.P.S.T. (Adj.)
(Close on Heat Rise)

S.P.D.T. (Adj.)

S.P.S.T. (Adj.)
(Open on Heat Rise)

S.P.D.T. (Adj.)
(With Aux. "OFF" Contacts)
(Typical Example)

S.P.S.T. (w/Internal Heater)
(Close on Heat Rise)

S.P.S.T. (w/Internal Heater)
(Open on Heat Rise)

MOTORS

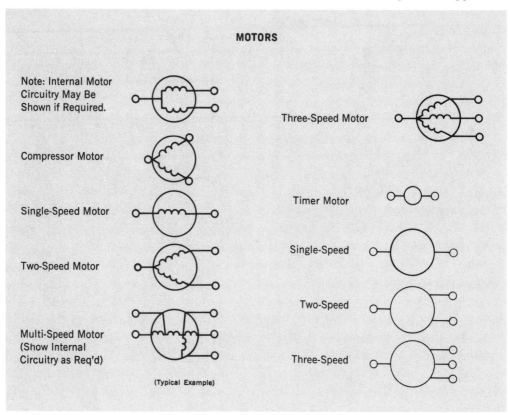

Note: Internal Motor Circuitry May Be Shown if Required.

Compressor Motor

Single-Speed Motor

Two-Speed Motor

Multi-Speed Motor (Show Internal Circuitry as Req'd)

(Typical Example)

Three-Speed Motor

Timer Motor

Single-Speed

Two-Speed

Three-Speed

LINES AND CONNECTIONS

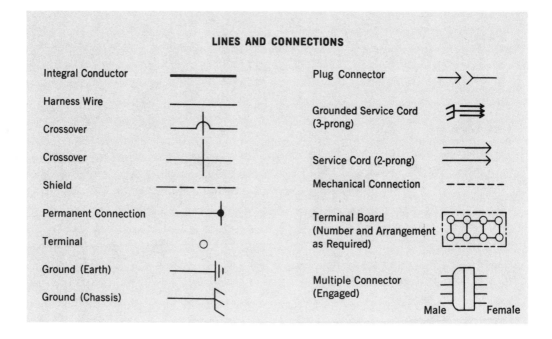

Integral Conductor

Harness Wire

Crossover

Crossover

Shield

Permanent Connection

Terminal

Ground (Earth)

Ground (Chassis)

Plug Connector

Grounded Service Cord (3-prong)

Service Cord (2-prong)

Mechanical Connection

Terminal Board (Number and Arrangement as Required)

Multiple Connector (Engaged)

Male   Female

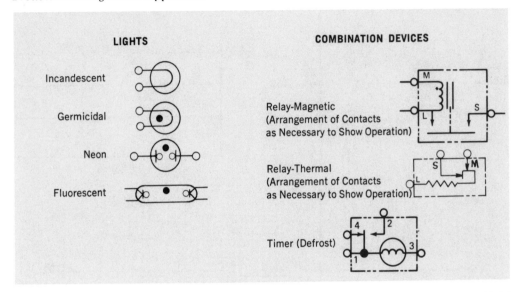

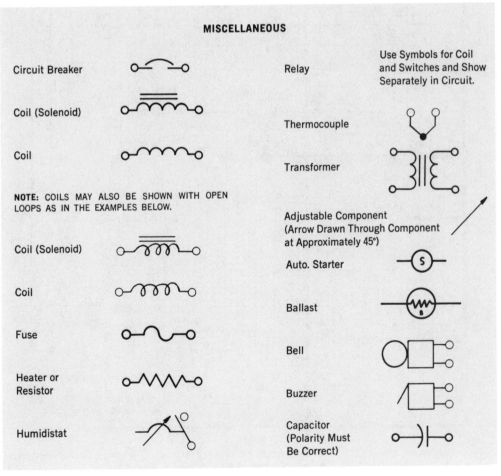

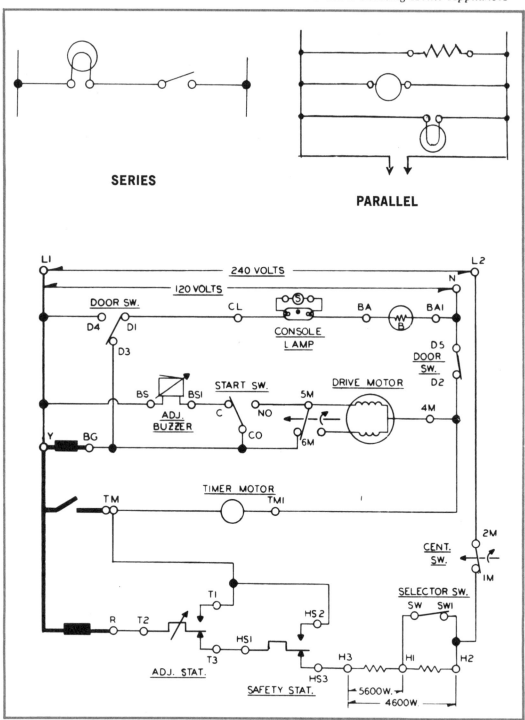

SERIES

PARALLEL

▲ *This typical wiring diagram is for an electric dryer. Every appliance complicated enough to require a wiring diagram has one attached in an out-of-sight location.*

Trouble-shooting Home Appliances

Switches and thermostats control the flow of electricity. Motors, heaters, lights, and solenoids use electricity to do work. A relay both uses and controls the current.

The two principal methods of connecting parts are "in series" and "in parallel." Most diagrams are a combination of these as shown in the electric dryer diagram.

The ways of wiring. A schematic wiring diagram shows, by symbols, the various parts that use electricity and how they are wired—electrically connected—to each other. This type of diagram is usually attached to an appliance and sometimes included in your owner's manual.

Don't let the size or complexity of a diagram, or the number of parts and wires worry you. Study it and follow each circuit, one at a time. Remember that there must always be a complete electrical path from one side of the input to the other.

Electrical failures. An electrical part may fail for either a mechanical or an electrical reason:

1. Switch parts may break, wear, or burn out.
2. Motors may develop bearing wear or "freezing."
3. A housing may crack.
4. A screw may vibrate loose.
5. Solenoid plungers may stick.
6. Contact points may stick and weld together.
7. A loose part may chafe the insulation or cut a wire.
8. A part may "burn out." That is, when it is overheated, a wire or a contact may melt thus breaking the electrical circuit. The part should be replaced.
9. A part may go "open circuit." That is, a wire or connection may break or a contact in a switch may fail to close. This can be repaired or replaced.
10. A part may "short-circuit." That is, an unexpected, unauthorized, or improper electrical connection may oc-

▶ *A volt-ohmmeter is the recommended tool for testing appliance electrical circuits.*

cur within a part. This diverts the flow of electricity from its proper path, drawing an excessive amount of current. It usually causes a fuse to blow or an overload protector to function. The short will have to be cleared and the part repaired or replaced, depending on the extent of damage.

11. A part may "ground." That is, there will be an insulation breakdown between the current carrying and the non-current carrying parts of an assembly. The part may remain operating but the user will get a shock from the appliance unless metal parts of the appliance are properly grounded.

All built-in appliances have provisions for grounding to a water pipe or some such metal conductor to earth. Many plug in appliances are now connected with a special three-wire cord, one terminal of which grounds through a special wire in the household's electrical circuit.

Remember these basic electrical failures, then realize that one may cause another. For example, a wire might chafe against a frame, eventually wearing the insulation to a degree that will allow the bare wire to "ground" on the frame. This may cause a "short circuit" that could "burn out" a switch, causing it to go "open" and giving the user a "shock" in the process.

▲ *A test light with two 120-volt lamps in series can be used to test either a 120- or 240-volt line to determine if a circuit is live. Use 15- or 25- watt lamps.*

Repairing connections. Most wires are attached to components with quick-disconnect-type terminals and connectors. A damaged terminal or connector should be replaced, soldering a wire to a terminal will work in a pinch but it is not recommended. This will not affect operation of the machine; but it will make things more difficult if the part has to be removed in the future.

Chafed wire insulation must be taped to protect it from being grounded and then the wire should be so positioned that the chafing won't happen again.

When disconnecting leads from the terminals, it is wise to make a sketch using a color code to remind you of the right terminals for each lead.

It often happens that the electrical supply cord breaks at the place where it connects to the attachment cap. This can occur through handling, aging (drying out), or accident. If the rest of the wire is all right and shows no signs of wear, cracking, drying out, etc., the best thing to do is to connect a new attachment cap.

Installing new cap on line cord. There is always more than one way to do a job, but when you attach a new cap to an appliance cord be sure to use an "underwriter's" knot. This is the approved means of providing "strain relief" so that any pulling of the cord will not tend to pull the wires from the screw terminals.

Using a test light. A great deal of checking can be done with a test light by connecting it to the terminals in parallel with the electricity-using part in question. If the bulb lights you know that electricity is available at the terminals of the part that is being tested and that any trouble is probably in the part itself. If the bulb does not light, you know that electricity is not reaching the part being tested; therefore, the trouble must be elsewhere.

When using a test light on a normal 115-volt appliance, a 115-volt bulb will do;

Trouble-shooting Home Appliances

but when working on an electric range, dryer, or any other 230-volt appliance, you must install a 230-volt bulb. At the higher voltage this bulb will light normally and at 115 volts it will light dimly. A 115-volt bulb used on 230-volt appliances will burn out.

Caution. You must know the complaint or reason for service before starting to look for trouble. This will tell you where to start testing and trouble-shooting. When using a test light to trouble-shoot an appliance, remember the power is turned on and you can get a shock. Be careful!

When working on an automatic appliance in which operations are controlled by a timer, make certain the timer is advanced to the circuit in question.

If you have a "healthy respect" for electricity and what it can do, it would be smart to use an ohmmeter or continuity tester with the power *disconnected* from the machine.

A simple continuity tester will show whether a circuit is continuous between two test points and indicate that electricity could flow there. This tester should be accurate enough to prove circuit "completeness" when the bulb lights.

A good volt-ohmmeter is a big help in circuit testing and will do much more than a test light. If you have one, use it.

Some areas of testing in electrical circuits require sensitive instruments. You would be wise to have such work tested by your qualified service man. When you reach the point where the equipment you have won't do the job, it is best to call for help from someone who has the special tools.

Who does the job? If, after having satisfied yourself that the trouble is not of a simple and observable nature, you still wish to continue further toward finding it yourself; you must answer some questions: Do you have the equipment to continue? Tools? Ability? Parts?

▲ *An appliance repairman's workbench.*

If you reach a "yes" decision, read carefully the basic information on the type of appliance you wish to repair. Also restudy the owner's manual for that appliance, supplied by the manufacturer.

Locate the wiring diagram, usually found on the access panel of appliances which are complex enough to require such information. Follow the steps outlined in the trouble-shooting charts until the failure is located.

Decide—again and finally—are you still going ahead with the job yourself? If you have gone this far to find out what the trouble is, you probably can. At the same time, some troubles way within the machine require special tools and equipment to repair.

Among items needing particular tools, equipment, and test apparatus are refrigerator compressor or evaporator, gear case assembly on a washer, bearings, an electric motor or coil needing rewinding, thermostats, timers, and and burner assemblies. This is the area where it is cheaper and safer to ask for professional help.   G.M.

See also: INDIVIDUAL APPLIANCE LISTINGS.

Finishing an Attic Room on a Small Budget

Unused attic space in your home can be converted economically into an attractive living area

△ This is the kind of rough attic that the home handyman can convert to attractive living space, at a cost of about one third of what a contractor would charge to do the work.

MANY OWNERS of small single houses find they lack a spare room for unexpected guests or for the children when the size of their family increases.

The home handyman can build a finished room at comparatively small expense if there is a rough attic in the house with a stairway, which is used now only for storage. Such was the case with this bungalow-type house that has a large unfinished attic and only five rooms on the first floor; an extra guest room was badly needed.

While house designs vary considerably, in layout and construction, the procedure outlined here can be used as a general guide to the work by modifying the plans as required to fit the individual house.

The cost for materials to build this attractive room was about one-third of the cost of having a contractor do the work.

There was no dormer on this house which, of course, would be desirable to admit added light and ventilation to the new room, but it was felt that the expense would not be justified in having one built by a professional carpenter. Therefore, this was not considered.

A large window facing west will provide good afternoon sunlight. With a similar window in the unfinished section, it is possible to get cross ventilation with both windows open, if the doors separating the two sections are left open.

This project called for framing off with studding an area 14x15 feet, not counting the space taken by the stairway and the closet. A partition divides the finished from the rough part. The chimney is in the rough section, and the soil pipe that extends up through the roof is enclosed in the closet wall. A door leads from the finished room to the closet and another door goes from the back wall of the closet into the storage area.

Most attics have a single flooring overlay over the joists. If one doesn't, then· it is necessary to lay some spruce boards for a flat, smooth sub-floor before putting up the studding. Later, hardboard is layed over the sub-floor and floor tiles are used for the finished floor.

First step is to lay out your room area, taking care to get the marked out space square. This can be done with the usual corner measurements, and snapping a chalk line guide on the floor.

Finishing an Attic Room on a Small Budget

A knee wall is required at two sides of the room which should be a minimum height of three feet. Short studs cut on an angle at one end should match the slope of the roof rafters. Minimum height of the ceiling should be about seven feet from the finished floor.

Collar beams are nailed to the rafters as the supports for the ceiling. Where the distance is only about four to five feet, 1x6-inch fir boards can be used for collar beams. Use 2x4 or 2x6-inch lumber for longer spans between nailing points on the rafters. These beams should be leveled, and their lower edges properly lined up to get a good level ceiling. Nail furring strips to the collar beams on 12-inch centers for the tiles used to finish off ceiling.

Use 2x3-inch studs in the dividing partition between the finished and unfinished areas since this partition carries no weight, or substitute 2x4s if preferred or required by a building code. The sole plate consists of furring strips which are nailed to the sub-flooring. Studding can be used for the sole plate at somewhat higher cost.

Put the studs up on two-foot centers so a standard sheet of four-foot wide wall board can be conveniently nailed in place. If more studs are desired locate them on 16-inch centers. Make sure all studs are installed level.

Short pieces of 2x3s are used for the knee wall. They are attached to the lower edges of the rafters to provide nailing points for the top ends of the partition studs where they come between rafters. These studs for the knee wall are cut at an angle and nailed to the existing rafters. There is a limited height for the door, due to the sloping rafters, but it is possible to use a 74-inch door.

Short pieces of furring, with end cleats, or 2x3s must be nailed between the knee wall studs where they are attached to the rafters for supports and to provide a nailing surface for the wallboard. Remember to use double-studding in the closet.

Install the heating outlets while the walls are still open. In this case the original contractor had carried a riser from the steam boiler up the side of the chimney to the attic floor line, where it was capped, thus providing for future expansion.

It was a simple job to remove the cap and extend the 1¼-inch pipe to the location for the new radiator. Measurements

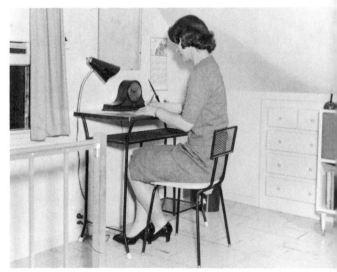

⋏ *Completed conversion, shown in these two photos, includes built-in bookcase (at left of room) and built-in chest of drawers (at right). Railing in background next to the stairwell was purchased as a unit from a department store.* ◄

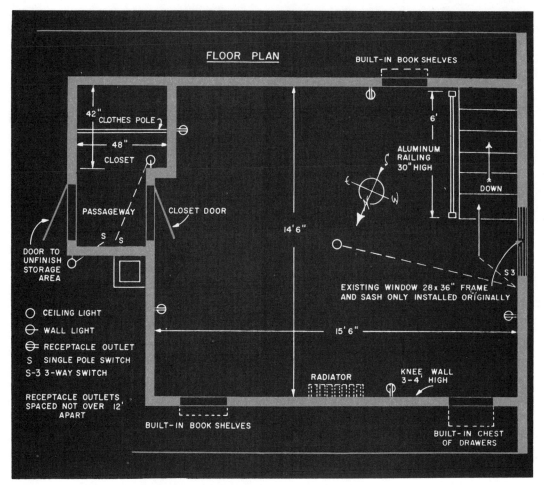

FLOOR PLAN

BUILT-IN BOOK SHELVES

42"
CLOTHES POLE

48"

CLOSET

PASSAGEWAY

S / S

CLOSET DOOR

DOOR TO
UNFINISH
STORAGE
AREA

6'

ALUMINUM
RAILING
30" HIGH

DOWN

14'6"

EXISTING WINDOW 28 x 36" FRAME
AND SASH ONLY INSTALLED ORIGINALLY

S 3

○ CEILING LIGHT
⊖ WALL LIGHT
⊖ RECEPTACLE OUTLET
S SINGLE POLE SWITCH
S-3 3-WAY SWITCH

RECEPTACLE OUTLETS
SPACED NOT OVER 12'
APART

15'6"

RADIATOR

KNEE WALL
3-4 HIGH

BUILT-IN BOOK SHELVES

BUILT-IN CHEST
OF DRAWERS

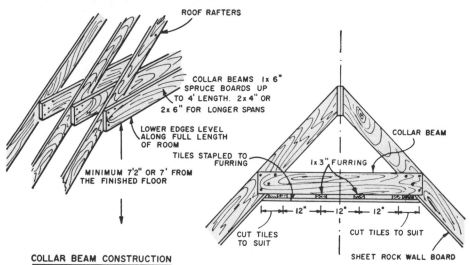

ROOF RAFTERS

COLLAR BEAMS 1 x 6"
SPRUCE BOARDS UP
TO 4' LENGTH. 2 x 4" OR
2 x 6" FOR LONGER SPANS

LOWER EDGES LEVEL
ALONG FULL LENGTH
OF ROOM

TILES STAPLED TO
FURRING

MINIMUM 7'2" OR 7' FROM
THE FINISHED FLOOR

COLLAR BEAM CONSTRUCTION

COLLAR BEAM

1 x 3" FURRING

12" — 12" — 12"

CUT TILES
TO SUIT

CUT TILES TO SUIT

SHEET ROCK WALL BOARD

Finishing an Attic Room on a Small Budget

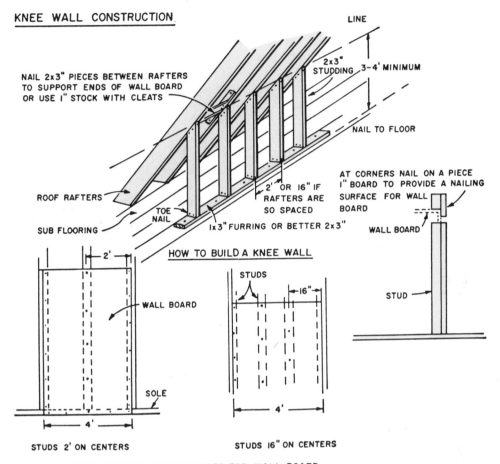

KNEE WALL CONSTRUCTION

NAIL 2x3" PIECES BETWEEN RAFTERS
TO SUPPORT ENDS OF WALL BOARD
OR USE 1" STOCK WITH CLEATS

LINE

2x3"
STUDDING 3-4' MINIMUM

NAIL TO FLOOR

ROOF RAFTERS

TOE
NAIL

SUB FLOORING

2' OR 16" IF
RAFTERS ARE
SO SPACED

1x3" FURRING OR BETTER 2x3"

AT CORNERS NAIL ON A PIECE
1" BOARD TO PROVIDE A NAILING
SURFACE FOR WALL
BOARD

WALL BOARD

STUD

HOW TO BUILD A KNEE WALL

WALL BOARD

SOLE

2'

4'

STUDS 2' ON CENTERS

STUDS

16"

4'

STUDS 16" ON CENTERS

HOW SUPPORTS ARE PROVIDED FOR WALL BOARD

were taken and the pipe cut and threaded at a local plumbing supply dealer.

We bought the radiator from a dealer in used plumbing supplies for about half of what a new one would cost. Select a radiator that's as clean as possible and is large enough to provide adequate heat.

In cases where there is no extension from the boiler provided for future use, or where another type of heating system exists, it is necessary to call in a heating man to do this part of the work for you. In some cases the extra piping or duct work can be brought up from the basement by running it through a closet. Any ex-posed duct or pipe can be completely covered with asbestos sheathing.

In any case, use insulation over the heating pipe to conserve the heat. The pipe should have a slight downward slant which allows condensed water to flow back to the boiler.

Electrical wiring, like heating, should be installed while the walls are still open. One way to bring power to the room is to run a new cable to the attic from the main fuse box. You might be able to snake it up next to the chimney. Another method: hook the attic system to the junction or fixture boxes of the wiring for the rooms below, especially if these boxes are in the ceiling. If you do use existing wiring, make certain you do not overload any circuits.

Insulation necessary. For maximum effectiveness, try to cut insulation to exact length required so you won't end up "patching" one channel with a series of small pieces. The thick fiberglass in the material used here ensures maximum effect, and the reflective aluminum foil serves both as a vapor barrier and to reflect heat back in the room in winter.

Attach insulation to the sides of the roof rafters with ⅜ or ½-inch staples that are placed every 12 inches. Staple length is determined by the hardness and condition of the rafters. Fold the edges of the paper over the front corners so that when the finished wallboard material is on, a good seal is provided.

Edges of the insulation may have to be cut a bit at points where projections exist to fit the material tightly and smoothly in place. In this house 23-inch insulation was

required for the roof because the rafters were on 24-inch centers. Some houses have rafters that are on 16-inch centers; 15-inch insulation should be used. With the 23-inch size, it took just about one roll to a bay in a continuous length.

One wall of the room was also insulated. The fiberglass was cut off at the top ends and stapled to the last roof rafter to make a tight and weatherproof barrier.

Variety of wall covering. After the insulation is securely fastened you can install the wallboard. Sheetrock makes a very suitable material if care is taken to make the joints as invisible as possible. It is also one of the lowest cost materials for the job.

Or you can use wood paneling with V grooves that is available in several attractive finishes and grains. However, it is necessary to add horizontal cross braces in your framing to support the panels properly. The cost of such paneling will be considerably higher.

In the interests of economy, sheetrock

▶ *Use level to check all studs for plumb. The doorways are framed with double studs. The doorway in the foreground is for the closet. The one beyond it is in the back of the closet and opens to the unfinished portion of the attic.*

Finishing an Attic Room on a Small Budget

▲ Fiberglass and aluminum foil insulation is held in place by staples driven into studs and rafters every 12 inches.

was used. This material is available in ⅜-inch thickness. The side edges taper slightly so the joint can be sealed without causing a seam that can be easily noticed.

A special plaster compound is troweled into the joint, then a strip of perforated tape pressed down into the plaster. More plaster is then applied over the tape, finishing it off smooth with the surrounding surface. If carefully done, the joints will be practically invisible and will not crack open later.

Plan storage areas. A built-in chest of drawers was installed in the knee wall which is one of the attractive features of the new room. These units can be purchased in lumber yards complete, all ready to fit in the opening provided in the wall. Install by nailing through the finish trim at the sides and into the studs. The one used

here is a 24-inch size, which fit between the knee wall studs.

Two built-in bookshelves were made up from one-inch pine stock and installed in the knee wall at opposite sides of the room. It was assembled with glue and finishing nails, with the shelves fitting in dadoes cut in the sides. The back is a piece of ⅛-inch *Masonite* hardboard. Finish nails were driven through the sides and into the studs. Pine trim was used to cover the raw edges of the cabinet.

Apply finish trim around the window, using materials commonly sold for this purpose by lumber yards. Originally, only the window frame and the two sash sections were in place in the rough attic.

Molding and ceiling tile. This finish trim consists of a stool and apron at the bottom of the window, and smooth stock for the sides and top. Install stop molding around

▲ Pine bookcase with hardboard back was designed to fit into opening between studs of knee-wall.

the sides and top so it lines up close to the lower sash to keep it in place.

Screws should be used for this molding so it can easily be removed to replace a broken window or broken sash cords. Fin-

CORNER DETAIL OF WINDOW

SHOWING RELATION OF FINISH MATERIAL
WITH NAMES

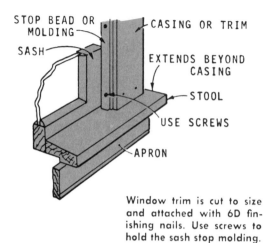

Window trim is cut to size
and attached with 6D fin-
ishing nails. Use screws to
hold the sash stop molding.

Finishing an Attic Room on a Small Budget

ish nails were used for the trim, but they
should not be driven all the way in with
a hammer. To avoid indenting on the
wood, use a nail set to drive them in the
last ⅛-inch and countersink the head just
below the surface.

To complete the ceiling, block tiles are
put up, which come in 12x12-inch squares
and are made of ½-inch insulating material that is painted on one side. The furring
strips were spaced so the ceiling tile could
be attached with $\frac{9}{16}$-inch staples.

Next step is to apply the rest of the
finish, which includes the door frame, the
finish molding, and nailing the base molding in place.

Frame the door opening. The door
frame was constructed from 1x3½-inch

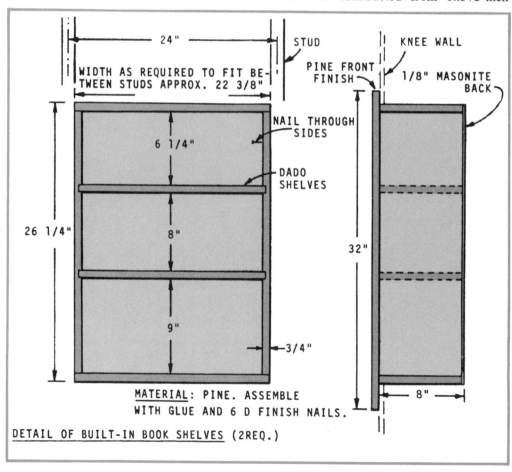

DETAIL OF BUILT-IN BOOK SHELVES (2REQ.)

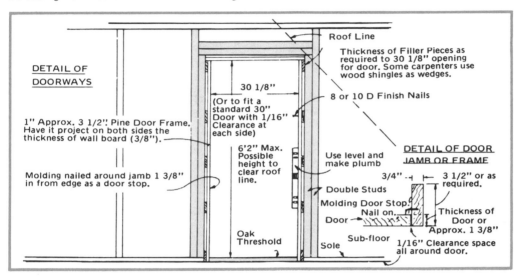

DETAIL OF
DOORWAYS

Roof Line

Thickness of Filler Pieces as
required to 30 1/8" opening
for door. Some carpenters use
wood shingles as wedges.

30 1/8"

(Or to fit a
standard 30"
Door with 1/16"
Clearance at
each side)

8 or 10 D Finish Nails

1" Approx. 3 1/2". Pine Door Frame.
Have it project on both sides the
thickness of wall board (3/8").

6'2" Max.
Possible
height to
clear roof
line.

Use level and
make plumb

DETAIL OF DOOR
JAMB OR FRAME

Molding nailed around jamb 1 3/8"
in from edge as a door stop.

3/4"   3 1/2" or as
required.

Double Studs

Molding Door Stop.
Nail on.

Door

Thickness of
Door or
Approx. 1 3/8"

Oak
Threshold

Sole

Sub-floor

1/16" Clearance space
all around door.

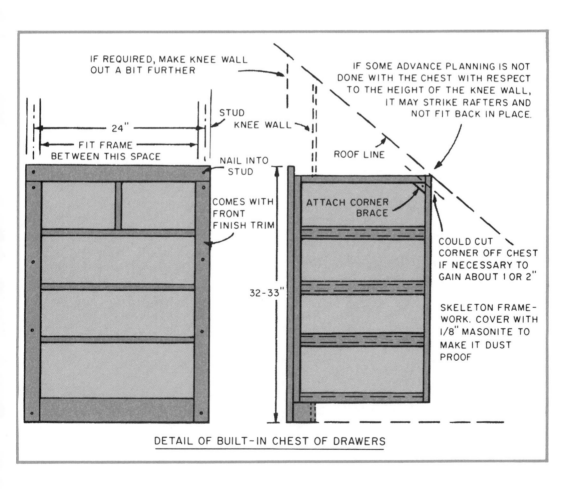

IF REQUIRED, MAKE KNEE WALL
OUT A BIT FURTHER

IF SOME ADVANCE PLANNING IS NOT
DONE WITH THE CHEST WITH RESPECT
TO THE HEIGHT OF THE KNEE WALL,
IT MAY STRIKE RAFTERS AND
NOT FIT BACK IN PLACE.

STUD
KNEE WALL

24"

FIT FRAME
BETWEEN THIS SPACE

ROOF LINE

NAIL INTO
STUD

COMES WITH
FRONT
FINISH TRIM

ATTACH CORNER
BRACE

COULD CUT
CORNER OFF CHEST
IF NECESSARY TO
GAIN ABOUT 1 OR 2"

32-33"

SKELETON FRAME-
WORK. COVER WITH
1/8" MASONITE TO
MAKE IT DUST
PROOF

DETAIL OF BUILT-IN CHEST OF DRAWERS

clear pine, with an oak threshold. The frame, or jamb as it sometimes called, should be wide enough so it is flush with the wallboard at both sides. If 2x3-inch studs are used, 3½-inch wide molding will be about the right size. For 2x4-inch studs, it will have to be wider.

Cut the stock to fit the opening so that with the addition of small blocks between it and the studs, a space will be provided to properly fit a standard 30-inch door. Figure the height to take the maximum height door that can get in. A standard 78-inch door will have to be cut down to fit.

Provide a stop for the door by nailing some molding around the sides and at the top of the jamb. Position this molding so it will allow the door to come flush with the edge of the jamb. Oak threshold stock can be easily purchased, and it should be cut and fitted between the lower ends of the jamb and nailed to the floor. Lay out this work to allow about 1/16-inch clearance all around the door so that it will open and close without binding in the door framework.

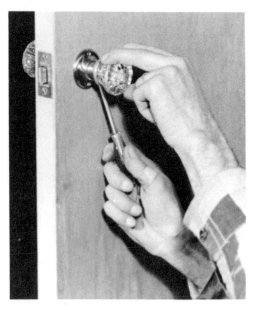

▲ *Tightening the doorknob setscrew is the final step in installing the door latch.*

Cut door to size. A flush door can be cut down to fit your needs. Clamp two pieces of 2x3-inch stock on the guide line, then use a sharp, fine-tooth hand saw to make the cut. Since these doors are hollow except at the sides and ends for a distance in of around 4 or 5 inches or so, cut across the hollow section and glue in a filler piece.

Make the filler piece from any soft wood stock of a thickness to fit in the hollow space, and about 2 or 3 inches wide. After the glue sets, the piece can be planed off flush.

Fit the door in the jamb by shaping it to get spacing all around for clearance, then hang it with two standard butt hinges that are set into a chiseled recess.

Position the hinges about 7 inches from each end of the door. Assemble the leaves with the pins, then place the door in the jamb. Insert a 1/16-inch piece of stock between the lower end of the door and the threshold for clearance, then mark the positions of the hinges on the jamb.

Chisel a recess for the top hinge leaves to bring them in flush and screw the leaves to the jamb. With the door again in place, insert the hinge pins and try it for a fit.

A little adjustment may be required, such as placing a piece of carboard in back of the hinges to shift the clearance to make it uniform, or perhaps a bit may have to be planed off the door if it strikes.

The door latch ordinarily used on a closet comes in a variety of types so you have many to choose from. They usually require that a large hole be bored in the door edge to pass the body of the latch, and another hole bored through the door at the point where the spindle is to pass through.

A latch plate must be fitted on the jamb. Let it in flush with a chisel at the correct marked spot, and use two screws to secure it. It's important to have the latch fit in the opening correctly to hold the door closed.

Finishing an Attic Room on a Small Budget

▶ Tiling gives an attractive finish to an attic room floor and is easy to maintain. Spread adhesive over small section of floor at a time with notched trowel, as shown, and set tiles in place.

▶ Self-adhesive tiles are a convenient alternative if you wish to avoid the extra work of using a flooring adhesive. Just peel off the paper backing on each tile...

▶ ...And set the tile in place. Press down firmly over surface of tile for a good bond. To cut edge pieces, warm tile then cut with scissors to premarked size.

Trim around the door can be applied now, using any type of molding finish desired. Carefully miter the corners, and keep edge back about ¼-inch from the side of the jamb. Set the nails in so the holes can be filled later.

Complete the finish by installing a base molding that goes all around the room. It can be about 2½ to 3 inches wide, as commonly used in many modern houses today. Countersink the finishing nails. They should be large enough so they hold the molding securely to the wallboard. Miter all corners.

Work in the closet consists of applying the wallboard to the studding in the same general manner as in the rest of the room. The door that leads out to the unfinished section is hung exactly the same way as the room door just completed. A base molding is also installed.

Paint suggestions. Use a brush or roller to apply two coats of flat paint to all the wallboard surfaces. The use of one of the water-base paints is suggested for easy application. This goes on well and dries to a uniform flat finish that is very attractive. It comes in a variety of colors, and in this case beige was selected.

The finish trim was painted with semi-gloss beige enamel. Before applying the enamel to the woodwork make sure all finish nails have been set and the filler used to cover the holes sanded down to provide a smooth and uniform surface.

Lay the flooring. One of the final major steps in the job is to lay the flooring. Sweep the floor and make sure there are no nails protruding or bits of material remaining. Hardboard, in ¼-inch thickness can be obtained from lumber yards in 4x4-foot sheets for easy handling, or cut to that size.

It should be nailed securely to hold the hardboard flat over the entire room. It may be necessary in a few spots to plane down some of the boards of the sub-floor or drive in some nails to level up the boards.

The tiles used were vinyl-asbestos which proved satisfactory, but one of the other available types may be used if desired.

Safety measures. One of the attractive features of the room is the aluminum stairway railing that was purchased from a department store in partially knockdown form. A few holes were required to be drilled in the posts during assembly, but otherwise it was quite complete. It was bolted down to the floor at the post flanges with lag screws. Railings come in six-foot lengths which was just right for our purpose, and the posts are 30 inches high.

A hand railing for the stairway was built from a length of one-inch electrician's aluminum conduit. Two hardwood plugs were used to cap the ends. Brackets commonly sold for use with wood hand rails were attached to the wall with wood screws that must turn into the studs.

Cost of new room. A breakdown in cost figures was approximately as follows:

Insulation	$200
Sheetrock	84
Ceiling tiles	12
2x3-inch studs, boards, and other lumber	90
Flush doors and all finish trim..	50
Floor tiles	80
Wiring and fixtures	70
Used radiator and piping	60
Built-in drawer chest	36
Pine for bookshelves	12
Aluminum railing	32
Hand rail and brackets	8
Hardboard floor underlay	30
Paint, nails and miscellaneous ..	30
	$794

The cost of course will vary somewhat in different localities and your sources of supply. A little shopping for prices among various firms dealing in building materials will often effect a saving.   H.P.S.

See also: WIRING, ELECTRICAL; INDIVIDUAL HOME ADDITIONS LISTINGS.

BLUEPRINT LANGUAGE

Here is a listing of abbreviations, terms and symbols most often used on blueprints and specifications noting materials, structure and conditions. You will find this list quite useful as reference after choosing a new home plan and ordering the working drawings

A.W.	Automatic Washer	Min.	Minimum
A.D.	Ash Dump	O.C.	On Centers
Cab.	Cabinet	O.H.	Overhead Door
Ceil.	Ceiling	Part.	Partition
¢	Center Line	P.C.	Pull Cord
C.I.	Cast Iron	Pl.	Plate
CL.	Closet	Plwd.	Plywood
Cl.W.P.	Clear White Pine	Prefab.	Prefabricated
Conc.	Concrete	R.C.	Reinforced Concrete
Contr.	Contractor	12 R	Twelve Risers (Vertical part of steps)
C.o.	Clean Out	S.	Sink
C.O.	Cased Opening	Sect.	Section
Cols.	Columns	Shr.	Shower
Corr.	Corrugated	Sl.	Sliding
Csmt.	Casement	T. C.	Terra Cotta
Cu. ft.	Cubic feet	Temp.	Tempered
D.A.	Double Acting Door	T.H.	Top Hinged
D.H.	Double Hung	T.O.	Trimmed Opening
Diag.	Diagonal	T & G	Tongued and Grooved
D & M	Dressed and Matched	Unex.	Unexcavated
Dn.	Down	V (or Vd)	V Groove
D.W.	Dish Washer	Vert.	Vertical
Exp.	Exposure	T.W.	To Weather
Ext.	Exterior	W.C.	Water Closet
F.A.I.	Fresh Air Intake	W.I.	Wrought Iron
F.	Fill	W.P.	Waterproof
Fin.	Finished	φ	Round
Ftgs.	Footings	Φ	Square foot
Fxd. (or F)	Fixed		
Ga.	Gauge		
Galv.	Galvanized		
Gl. (Glazed)	Glass		
Hd. Rm.	Head Room		
Hor. (Horiz.)	Horizontal		
H.T.	House Trap		
Htr.	Heater		
L.	Angle Iron		
L. (Lin.)	Linen		
Lav.	Lavatory		
Lino.	Linoleum		
L.T.	Laundry Tub (Or Trap)		
Lts.	Lights (Glass Areas)		
M.C.	Medicine Cabinet		

ELECTRICAL SYMBOLS

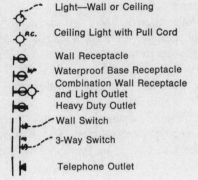

Light—Wall or Ceiling

Ceiling Light with Pull Cord

Wall Receptacle

Waterproof Base Receptacle

Combination Wall Receptacle and Light Outlet

Heavy Duty Outlet

Wall Switch

3-Way Switch

Telephone Outlet

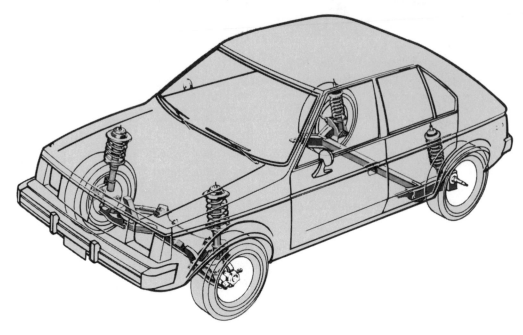

Maintenance Tips for Front-wheel Drive

Escalating prices and service charges make home auto care pay off

IT TOOK MORE THAN 20 YEARS for the front-drive/transverse-engine layout of the tiny British Mini—a brick riding on four doughnuts—to become the standard automobile configuration of the world. When first introduced in 1957, Sir Alec Issigonis's crosswise engine driving the front wheels was a radical layout. By the early 1980s, though, most of the newer small car designs dictated by high fuel prices followed just this form. Front-wheel drive (FWD) had arrived.

Along with the new configuration, the new front-wheel-drive cars came into a vastly different automotive world than their rear-drive predecessors. The home mechanics who worked on those cars often did so from interest and enthusiasm as well as from a desire to save money. More of

today's home mechanics have become involved in car repair to keep fuel mileage as high as possible and reduce repair or maintenance bills. With professional shops charging rates as high as $40 per hour, home auto repair has never paid off better.

Front-drive cars do all the same things as the long-familiar rear-drive models that preceded them. Therefore, most maintenance operations are basically very similar. The only major differences are the constant velocity universal joints that allow the front wheels to steer as well as drive, and an electric fan in the cooling system in place of the belt-driven fan used with a fore-and-aft engine mounting.

Otherwise, most maintenance and repair requirements apply to both the once-conventional rear-wheel-drive and front-wheel-

Maintenance Tips for Front-wheel Drive

◄ *The strut mount on VW Rabbit family should have about 3/16-inch gap between plate and rubber, not nearly ⁵/₈-inch as on this 40,000-mile car. Should be replaced.*

drive layouts equally. They vary slightly from one make to another, and with the type of engine installed. Diesels, however, require different kinds of care than do gasoline engines. Still, getting the most out of your front-wheel-drive car boils down to performing the required maintenance on or ahead of schedule and then making repairs or replacements when something does break.

Know your car. Your first line of defense against car trouble is to know what your car requires and when. This comes in the owner's manual and in the workshop manual. If you are serious about doing your own car maintenance, you need both. You may also want to get a do-it-yourself manual that covers specific procedures for the make and model of car you own. Before buying one, though, check it carefully to make certain it contains really helpful information and is not simply a rehash of a workshop manual.

Maintenance prevents most unexpected troubles, usually makes parts last longer than they otherwise might, improves fuel economy, and makes the car run better. It starts with a walk-around inspection similar to the pre-flight check a pilot gives

► *Prick punch upper camber-adjusting bolt and strut so the parts can be reassembled in their original positions so as not to change original settings. This could save alignment job, though realignment may still be needed.*

his airplane before flying it. With a car, though, this can be a once-a-week effort that takes about five minutes. Then there are the maintenance procedures required by the car maker—usually at specified mileage or time intervals. These include changing the oil and filter, making other minor adjustments or parts replacements, and inspecting parts that wear—such as brakes. Scheduled maintenance is often performed by mechanics in training and is both possible and worthwhile for beginning home mechanics. The time and tools required vary, but a Saturday afternoon should suffice for most of it, and the tools pay for themselves in just one or two jobs. What's more, you get the job done at your convenience without having to wait around for your turn or leave the car for a whole day to get two hours' work done on it.

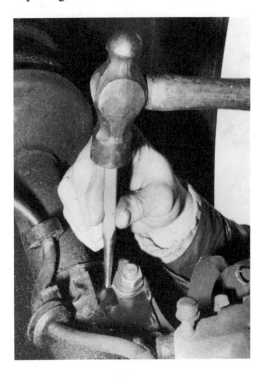

You may end up saving time as well as money on do-it-yourself maintenance.

Repairs on front-wheel-drive cars are usually no more difficult than on rear-drive types, just different. You reach the spark plugs on the front of the engine if it's a front-drive rather than from the side, but the plugs themselves are the same. We will cover replacing a rubber boot that protects the constant velocity joint in the front-drive axle and changing the shock absorber built into the MacPherson strut suspension used on most front-drive cars. The electric cooling fan rarely gives trouble and is covered in the car's workshop manual.

Walk-around inspection. Fuel, air, oil, water, water, plus brake fluid and windshield washer solvent are what you check in your weekly preflight. Fuel in the tank. Air in the tires (use your own gauge, those in many service stations are grossly inaccurate), and run a hand over the tread

▲ *Machine shop's spring compressor, powered by compressed air, makes it easy and safe to disassemble MacPherson struts and reassemble with new parts. Tools to do it at home would cost more than having shop do it.*

▼ *Removing two nuts at top and two studs at bottom lets you lift out front strut assembly. Oil indicates failed seal and explains lack of damping action.*

to feel for uneven wear patterns caused by misaligned wheels. Oil level on the engine dipstick. Water (or antifreeze) level in the radiator or translucent coolant overflow reservoir. Water level in the battery (if yours has caps). Brake fluid level in the master cylinder reservoir. Washer solvent level in the translucent bottle under the hood. Press your thumb against the drive belt or belts to check tension (about ½-inch deflection is right). Eyeball or touch (with the engine cool) radiator hose connections to check for slow leaks. Check lights for burned-out bulbs, and you are done.

Periodic maintenance requirements for front-wheel-drive cars are pretty similar to those for rear-drive cars. However, you need to make an extra check. While you are under the car to drain the oil (and change the oil filter if it cannot be reached from above, as it cannot on the VW Rabbit and Chrysler Omni-Horizon), run a hand over the bellowslike rubber boot at the end of each front-drive axle. You are looking for traces of grease and hoping you won't find any. Black grease on the boot means that it cracked or something you ran over poked a hole in it. If this has happened, either have the boot replaced or change it yourself as soon as possible. If you do not, road dirt and water will get into the joint and destroy it. Should this happen, you will need a new joint or perhaps an exchange drive axle costing well over $100.

Changing a front axle boot is a messy job that takes most of an afternoon. A dealer usually charges $50 or more for the job. The boot itself cost less than $10. You will probably need some special tools —a big socket for the large nut on the outside of the front-drive axle, and possibly snap ring pliers to take the joint apart so you can slip the new boot over the end of the axle. If the end is splined (ridged), cover the sharp edges with masking tape so they do not cut the new boot as you slip it in place. Use new metal clamps to secure the ends of the boot. You need two, a small one for the end on the axle shaft and a large one for the outside of the joint.

Doing the job requires wrenches big enough to unscrew the nut on the end of the front-drive axle shaft. With it loose, jack and safely support the car so you can remove the whole shaft with the bad boot. VWs and Omni-Horizons require a special tool for the inside fasteners that hold the axle's inner joint to the transaxle. Some other models require removing the lower mounting bolts from the MacPherson strut to gain enough clearance to remove the axle shaft from the front hub.

You will also need special grease for the constant velocity joint which should be carefully cleaned and repacked if there is any trace of grit in the grease from the hole in the boot. If the joint is worn or shows any radial play that you can feel, if the balls are pitted or spalled (chipped) or if the outer housings are damaged or discolored, the joint is near failure. Re-

▲ Rear strut has been reassembled in spring compressor with new Koni shock insert. Retaining nut is being tightened. Second nut, tightened against the first, locks the assembly together to prevent possible loosening.

place it while you have the axle out of the car.

Some constant velocity joints are pressed onto the axle and must be removed or installed by a machine shop with the proper press. Hammering on it will not do a satisfactory job. Taking the axle to the shop, though, is a lot cheaper than taking the whole car in and paying full shop rates to have them take out the axle, replace the joint, and then reinstall it.

This procedure demonstrates one of the best ways to handle major do-it-yourself jobs on any car, whether it has front- or rear-wheel drive—do the time-consuming part of the job yourself and then take the assembly needing repairs to a shop which has the special tools to fix it right. Then you get back a clean, rebuilt part which you can usually reinstall much more easily than the rusted-in-place part you struggled to remove.

The same technique also works for the other major repair frequently required by

Maintenance Tips for Front-wheel Drive

◄ *Reassembled rear strut with new insert takes less than ten minutes to reinstall in your car— with one top nut and one bottom bolt. Removing and reinstalling strut yourself saves taking the whole car in for the repair.*

front-drive cars—upgrading a tired Mac-Pherson strut. These are the main spring-shock-absorber-suspension assemblies that support the front wheels of most small cars, with or without front-drive. Removing them from the car is a quick and easy job that you can do yourself. The tricky part on some models is to mark the lower camber-adjusting bolts before removal so they can be reinstalled at the same settings. The workshop manual gives details on this job. (But even if you are not certain you have reinstalled the camber bolts correctly, the new struts or strut inserts will probably change the front end alignment enough to warrant having it checked and adjusted anyway.)

Once a MacPherson strut assembly is removed from your car, the disassembling and reassembling with new parts is best left to a machine shop with special equipment as it is a difficult and potentially dangerous job. Machine shop charge, as of 1982, runs about $15 per strut and is well worth it. Purchasing machinery and tools to do the job would cost you more.

A very real advantage of removing the strut assembly yourself and taking it and new parts to a shop for the necessary work means that you get to choose the brand and type of replacement strut or insert. If you take the car to a dealer, you will pay top dollar for an original equipment replacement that will not be any better than the one that failed. On many makes of cars, shock absorbers and MacPherson struts are designed to give a soft ride when the car is new so the customer will buy it. Once worn, they quickly become much too soft. By buying high quality inserts or replacements—often listed as sports or heavy duty types—you can greatly improve the handling and surefootedness of your car. Installing Koni inserts on a VW Rabbit made the car both handle and ride better at 40,000 miles than it did when new. Premium strut inserts like these may cost almost twice as much as lesser replacements, but they more than pay for themselves over the long term because they should not require replacement again. Konis have frequently given 100,000 or more miles of service compared with 10,000 to 30,000 for original equipment.

Most other repairs on front-wheel-drive cars are similar to the same jobs on rear-drive cars. Brakes are brakes, and tuneup doesn't change because the engine drives the front wheels instead of the rears.

Caring for a front-drive is well within the capability of most do-it-yourself mechanics. It's all a matter of using common sense and going by the book for your specific car make and model. And, unlike rear-wheel drive, remember to put your best tires on those front wheels. They do most of the work of driving, steering, and stopping the car; the rears are just along for the ride.

> *Lincoln Versailles.*

The Automobile in the Electronics Age

What electronics can do to make your car more pollution-free, more efficient and even more accident-free

YOUR AUTOMOBILE ALREADY contains many electronic systems, either as standard production items or as regular production options. Things such as automatic speed control, electronic fuel injection, ignition timing control and automatic headlight dimmers. But the auto industry admits there is still a long way to go in development of electronic gear that will make your car more pollution-free, more efficient and even more accident-free.

Electronics is going to change the cost, the performance and maybe even the appearance of cars but one thing it is not likely to replace is you, the driver. Automatically controlled and guided personal automobiles, programmed by computer to go from one random place to another, are not likely to be owned by anyone now alive, even though they are technically feasible right now.

However, the rush is on by Detroit, the major overseas companies, and the vendors of electronics gear to begin to gain for the automobile the benefits of the electronics age.

Why this great interest all of a sudden? A combination of reasons. Until now the auto industry has not been under such severe pressure to produce cars that squeeze the final bit of mileage out of each drop of gas while also removing the final traces of pollutants.

And, perhaps equally important, the auto industry needs something new besides styling to intrigue an increasingly sophisticated new-car-buying public. The fact is that new cars cost so much that already people are holding onto their old ones an extra year on the average. And, given the additional fact that more and more of us are taking four years to pay off a car, Detroit is worried that people will keep their wheels for five years or more instead of just over three.

That explains the interest in electronic gear. But perhaps the car companies have an excuse, too, for not jumping into electronics. If just one electronic component that's in, say a Chevrolet, proves faulty, imagine the number of inoperable cars!

Detroit, therefore, has been worried about the reliability of electronic components and systems. Automobiles are a poor environment for electronic circuitry. They offer a combination of much vibration and wide variations in temperature and humid-

ity. Moreover, any automotive electronic circuitry must be protected from outside electrical interference.

Electronic control systems use circuitry sensitive to current and voltage change. That's how they work. They either detect and amplify a signal or act when a signal stops. A nearby diathermy machine may send signals that can be picked up and make a tachometer needle go wild or warning lights go on or, more dangerous, electronically controlled brakes act unstable.

▼ *The Ford-developed interactive Electronic Engine Control (EEC) controls both engine spark timing and exhaust gas recirculation. Heart of the system is a solid-state module with a digital microprocessor and other custom-designed integrated circuits. Standard power-plant for the Versailles, the system provides emissions-control, fuel economy and performance benefits.*

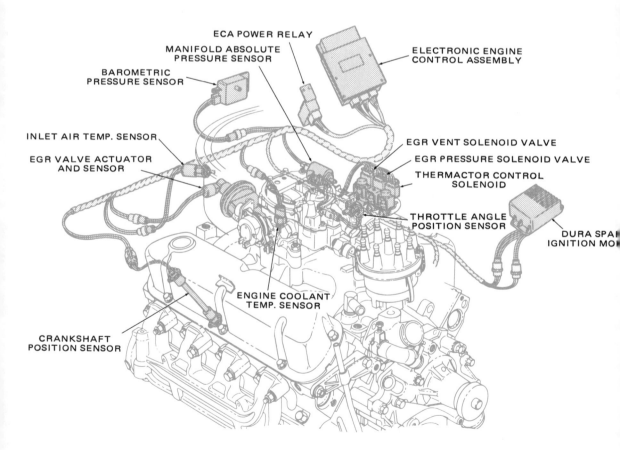

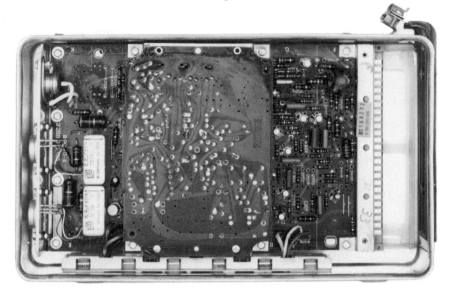

◄ *Cover plate is removed to reveal some of the more than 250 transistors and other electronic components which go into computers in fuel injection systems of some VW models. The unit senses engine requirements under constantly changing conditions and maintains a fully controlled flow of fuel to the cylinders, giving them just the right amount of gasoline under all kinds of operating conditions.*

What it takes to forestall this is more careful shielding and circuit design.

It is not desirable to try to gather all the electronics in a car into a single centrally located computer even though it would be less expensive. Longer connecting leads mean increased possibility of external interference. This has an effect upon each unit's own performance and upon other electronic devices as well. (VW was one of the first if not the first to install a "little black box" on its cars—electronic ignition.)

Instead of the single computer, it is recommended that the electronics be gathered into three separate packages: one near the driver, another in the engine compartment and a third—for such things as braking or speed control devices—beneath the rear seat.

Among electronic components of the near future, GM sees automatic braking and an inexpensive electronic system to prevent drunks from operating their cars. Currently existing radar braking not only is costly but more importantly lacks good discrimination between non-dangerous and dangerous obstacles. The automatic brakes take over suddenly, for instance, when a driver in full control may turn a sharp corner where allowance has been made for an old tree to grow to the curb. But GM believes that these problems can be solved.

The electronic anti-drunk systems are closer, however, since they work on the idea that the operator must punch out a number sequence before the ignition key can be turned.

Any number of anti-pollution systems utilize electronics and that also will be common until car researchers reach their main goal of eliminating the need for add-ons like catalytic mufflers and EGR by cleaning up the engine internally. For instance, Volvo has been using its Lambda-sond three-way catalytic system in California on 240 series cars.

The Lambda-sond system, as employed by Volvo, involves an oxygen sensor in the exhaust stream, an electronic control box, an air flow sensor to regulate fuel distribution and two other components—Volvo's three-way catalytic muffler which uses noble metals to render various pollutants harmless, and mechanical fuel injection.

The oxygen sensor (Lambda-sond in Swedish) feeds the ratio of oxygen in the exhaust into a microprocessor or electronic control unit. The ratio of oxygen is vital because the three-way catalyst needs the right diet to reduce carbon monoxide, hydrocarbons and oxygen nitrides simultaneously (It uses the oxygen in the CO to reduce the NOX, thereby turning the CO into harmless CO_2 and helping to burn the HC).

Chrysler thinks the carburetor will be the next familiar part to fall to an electronic successor—a successor more reliable, longer lasting and more accurate than any carburetor now known. It also talks of electronic transmissions which would further reduce weight and increase reliability. And the company points out that future electronic-oriented cars will be easier to service—just pull out the offending electronic module after you have identified it with plugged-in diagnostic aids and install a new one.

Actually, Chrysler and everyone else is awaiting the design or invention of a better absolute pressure sensor. When that comes —a sensor even more precise than today's marvels which react to pressures so small as to be incomprehensible to the layman— the whole electronics scene will take a giant step forward.

How about an instrument panel which can provide the car's occupants with instantaneous answers to hundreds of questions or even act as a combination secretary and reminder? The driver or passenger would program the unit for a flashing reminder that ten minutes from now his kids are to be picked up.

Or the dash might provide a running tab on expense account items such as tolls or gas mileage.

Or it might supply readouts on spark timing, intake manifold vacuum, engine torque, water temperature or simply tell you to get the car to a repair man quickly because trouble is impending.

There could be even separate display panels for driver and passenger and separate programming.

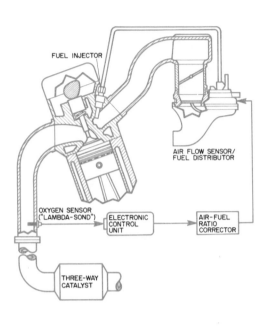

▲ *This diagram shows the major components of the Volvo Lambda-sond three-way catalytic converter emissions control system.*

Auto makers and their suppliers are working hard on that precisely because it is very marketable and because it solves problems. They are working equally hard on multiplex systems to contain much of the automobile's complex wiring system in a single cable.

And, if costs can be controlled, you might even get the kind of navigation devices which tell you where you are at any given point in your pre-programmed journey. This will help you choose the quickest route by avoiding traffic tie-ups and might even deter thieves.

One exciting automotive computer on the market is the Cadillac Seville "Tripmaster." It shows you the average speed at which you are driving and if you tell it how far away your destination is, it will read out your estimated time of arrival. It also lets you know your fuel consumption and computes, on command, the number of miles you can still travel on the fuel left in your tank.   **B.F.**

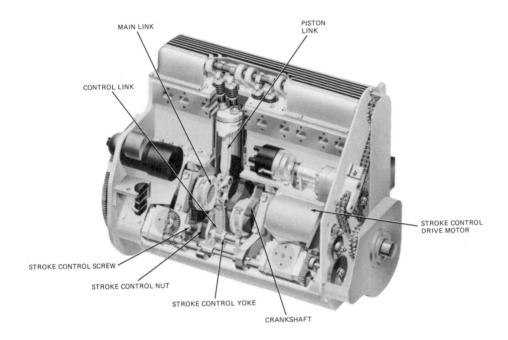

MAIN LINK

PISTON LINK

CONTROL LINK

STROKE CONTROL DRIVE MOTOR

STROKE CONTROL SCREW

STROKE CONTROL NUT

STROKE CONTROL YOKE

CRANKSHAFT

Variable Displacement Engines

Retain the full power
of your engine
for when it is needed

EVERY TIME SOMEONE wants to administer the last rites to the good old piston engine that millions of mechanics know and understand, someone else comes along to give it a new lease on life. And make no mistake: the good old piston engine has been under tremendous pressure as carmakers the world over have tried to figure out how to make it run clean without a lot of add-on paraphernalia and yet run on the smallest possible amount of ever more expensive gasoline.

Economy especially is a difficult problem because, with the threat of gas shortages eased by higher prices, great numbers of Americans have indicated that they prefer cars that are larger than those normal in the rest of the world. The obvious way to get more miles per gallon—subcompact size cars—does not seem to be the answer for the United States.

So, faced with government mandates to meet miles per gallon standards and public apathy toward American-made subcompacts, the car companies have been surveying alternatives like the diesel and other more radical solutions. Some scientists have arrived separately at a similar answer—an engine in which displacement varies according to the job that must be done. And others are working on still another possibility—a variable piston.

Your car's V-8 engine hardly ever needs its maximum torque or horsepower if it is a standard size vehicle. In fact, it hardly uses more than half its available power even when it is starting, accelerating to street speeds, climbing any but the steepest hills, passing, or carrying its full complement of passengers.

So why not retain the full power for when it's needed and find some way to fuel only that part of the engine's capacity that is wanted when you are, for instance,

TOP DEAD CENTER

BOTTOM DEAD CENTER

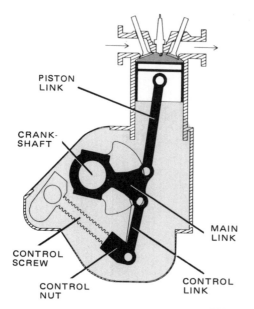

PISTON
LINK

CRANK-
SHAFT

CONTROL
SCREW

CONTROL
NUT

MAIN
LINK

CONTROL
LINK

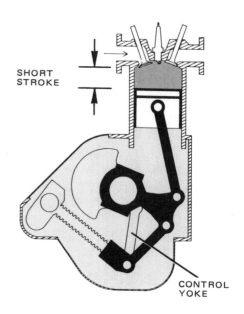

SHORT
STROKE

CONTROL
YOKE

SMALL DISPLACEMENT

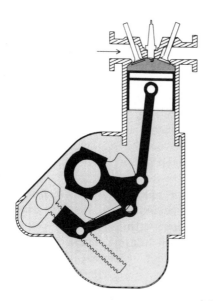

LONG
STROKE

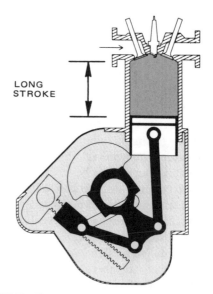

LARGE DISPLACEMENT

▲ *A variable displacement engine is shown in operation. Top drawings illustrate engine with displacement at its minimum for top dead cen-* *ter and bottom dead center positions. Bottom drawings show displacement at maximum for top dead center and bottom dead center positions.*

cruising along at moderate speeds or crawling in heavy traffic?

Ford scientists decided the quickest way to do this was by varying the number of cylinders in operation. If the engine is a six, have some kind of control which shuts off three; if the engine is a V-8, let the control shut off four. But this was easier said than done. Until electronic sensors came along to permit the use of a minicomputer, letting the engine know when to switch cylinders on and off was difficult and expensive.

It is less difficult now and less expensive, but Ford will use its "valve selector" mechanisms first on a small truck engine in 1979 or late 1978. You can expect what Ford calls Dual Displacement engines soon afterward on cars. Savings of 10 to 20 percent in miles per gallon are projected depending upon such usual variables as driving patterns and car use. This might be enough for Ford to meet fuel economy standards which begin to get really difficult by 1980—and meet them with larger-than-subcompact cars which predominate in its model mix.

The Ford DD engine has few changes from the conventional. Half the cylinders are equipped with solenoids which can shut these cylinders off if there is no demand for them.

The question of demand is answered via sensors monitoring transmission gear, throttle opening, engine load and speed, and temperature. This information is fed into a minicomputer or microprocessor which then may—or may not—signal the solenoids to mechanically actuate the valve selectors. It's that simple since the crankshaft already is turning. Of course, no one is saying much about crankshaft design or about the fact that such dual displacement setups may dictate other engine designs more suited to the dual arrangement.

Variable displacement is a fundamental rethinking of the good old conventional powerplant. The unique feature of the en-

gine, invented by a Sandia engineer, is a mechanical linkage enabling the driver to change automatically the length of the piston stroke, thus changing the displacement. By doing so, the driver is adjusting the engine's horsepower to meet varying driving demands.

Varying engine displacement (or cubic inch capacity) eliminates the need for a throttle, a major cause of inefficiency in conventional engines. In one engine, the throttle remains wide open except when the engine is idling.

Since this is a small displacement engine at low loads and gets larger only as loads increase, the gas mileage gain should be most dramatic when the vehicle is moving at a steady speed, not accelerating or climbing a grade. The estimates are that a mid-size car using a mature version of this engine should get 40 percent better gas mileage than a conventionally-powered identical car.

Of course, all these estimates are based on computer projections and dyno testing of the lone prototype in existence. This prototype is a five-cylinder engine with displacement varying from 43 to 190 cubic inches as the piston stroke changes from one to 4¼ inches. It has a maximum horsepower of about 100. Even this engine, which is several years from maturity, gets better gas mileage—30 percent better not counting emission controls—than its conventional counterpart in either highway or city driving simulations.

The inventor believes the additional refinements, already identified, will offset any penalty imposed by emission controls.

Here's how the engine differs from a conventional piston powerplant. In a conventional engine a single connecting rod transfers power from the piston to the crankshaft; the variable displacement engine adds additional links which also control piston travel. How far the piston travels is controlled by a mechanism on the accel-

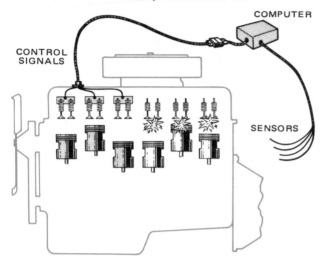

COMPUTER

CONTROL
SIGNALS

SENSORS

▲ The dual displacement engine is an important development for improved fuel economy. Only three of the engine's six cylinders operate automatically when power demands are minimal. All six cylinders come back into action instantaneously when the driver calls for them, as in passing or hill-climbing.

erator. In other words, if the driver pushes the pedal hard (steps on the gas) the engine will react much like other vehicles; the difference is that the conventional engine adjusts to power demands via the throttle and the carburetor while in the variable displacement engine the pedal adjusts the piston stroke.

How does this engine save gas? In conventional engines the maximum horsepower is determined largely by the cylinder volume displaced by the pistons, a volume which never varies. So when less than full power is needed—which is most of the time—the carburetor is throttled to reduce the amount of air/fuel mixture reaching the cylinders cutting engine efficiency. Since even a relatively heavy car needs only about 30 horsepower for level road cruising at 60 mph, according to the Sandia scientists, the answer is a variable displacement engine which, since the throttle is open, operates at good efficiency at whatever displacement is needed to do the job.

Sandia Laboratories is a government lab affiliated with the Energy Research and Development Administration. ERDA has filed

Variable Displacement Engines

patents on the engine which, by the time you read this, may be tooling around in a car in the next phase of development, all fitted out with catalytic mufflers and other emission equipment.

Even if everything goes exceptionally smoothly and Detroit picks up on the design, estimates are that the earliest you will see this in a car you buy is 1983. But that would be in plenty of time to help what by then will be a cost crunch for gasoline.

Chrysler and Teledyne Continental Motors, which makes military engines, are both working on lightweight diesels. The reason the diesel now built is so heavy is to withstand the tremendous pressures inside. Chrysler is working on ways to reduce the very high pressure at combustion, thus reducing the heavy structure and, perhaps, improving fuel economy even more.

Teledyne developed a unique variable compression ratio piston for diesel engines. Using this invention, it was able to increase the performance output of the test diesel by 50 percent without undue stress. The effect of this is to eliminate the slow acceleration of the diesel without using an expensive trick transmission.

The VCR piston is really an upper piston inside a lower piston. The upper piston is supported by a film of oil. A check valve controls the amount of oil between the pistons according to how much load the engine is subjected to. And the amount of oil between the pistons determines the operating ratio since the lower piston is forced down by more oil.

But Teledyne now has gone beyond the VCR piston in improving the diesel to meet the parameters of the 1980s in passenger cars. It has added turbocharging and variable injection timing. With modifications, the engine will be producible in large quantities on a car production line and would be similar in both size and weight to a comparable gasoline engine such as the American Motors 232 CID six cylinder.